ONCE UPON A LIFE

By
Gary F. Prestipino

Bloomington, IN Milton Keynes, UK

authorHOUSE™

AuthorHouse™
1663 Liberty Drive, Suite 200
Bloomington, IN 47403
www.authorhouse.com
Phone: 1-800-839-8640

AuthorHouse™ UK Ltd.
500 Avebury Boulevard
Central Milton Keynes, MK9 2BE
www.authorhouse.co.uk
Phone: 08001974150

This book is a work of non-fiction. Unless otherwise noted, the author and the publisher make no explicit guarantees as to the accuracy of the information contained in this book and in some cases, names of people and places have been altered to protect their privacy.

First published by AuthorHouse 2/27/2006

ISBN: 1-4259-1589-2 (sc)
ISBN: 1-4259-1590-6 (dj)

Printed in the United States of America
Bloomington, Indiana

This book is printed on acid-free paper.

I dedicate this book to my family and all the memories they have provided me in my life.

Acknowledgments

I'd like to acknowledge the following people:

I want to give a special dedication to my dad, who has inspired me to tell my stories.

My mom, who has always been there for me, and never judges me.

My grandpa Jim for telling me all about his life.

Monique, this book is for you and the future, never forget.

Janet, my wife, who has stood by and encouraged me every step of the way.

Contents

Introduction

Did you ever think you were special, that your life was unusually different from most people? I believe things happen to people for a reason. I don't know why I was chosen to share my life and family with you, but I was. It's impossible for other people to understand what you're thinking, why you feel one way or another about something important or not important. Well, I've always felt like that. I seemed to have a sense of what people are thinking, a respect for older people, and a love for the young. People never stop to listen to someone else's opinion or an interesting story. A story is either true or fictional; it means that this event actually happened or someone imagined it happened and is able to tell it like it was fact. When you think about it, does it really matter if it really happened? After the event took place, it's over, and the way you tell the story is what lives forever. Did you know I've learned more about life from my parents and grandparents than any book or documentary could have ever? I am going to attempt to tell my stories of events that have either happened to me personally, to a family member, or a friend. All of these stories are based on true events. I cannot confirm how many of them have been exaggerated over the years, but it wouldn't be a story if there wasn't some sort of exaggeration. The thing about most of these stories is that while I was hearing them firsthand, I can actually say I felt like I was right smack in the middle of it. It could be because I have traveled back in time on many occasions, sometimes not at the most convenient of times. To date, I have lived a remarkable life. I have traveled around the world in present and past times, I have met the most amazing people, and have witnessed memorable and not-so-memorable events. I have always had closeness to my family, especially my grandfather. I could feel the cold air of a 1922 winter, riding a milk truck over the Brooklyn Bridge, running through a forest barefoot to get a doctor for an ailing father, working deep in the coal mines in Scranton, Pennsylvania, watching baseball under the lights in a Negro League baseball exhibition game, seeing my parents meet for the first time in upstate New York, Catskill in 1950, or actually reliving a memorable event in my own life, the first time I hit a baseball. Baseball is a way of life; it's amazing how a person who died twenty years before I was born has such a connection with me. I could swear I saw Babe Ruth in person. There are many moments in my life where I cannot account for lost time and past events; whether or not I actually went back in time, or I have such a strong connection to my family past and extraordinary events that it all blends into one life. There have been minutes of my present life where I have traveled to another point in time. Most of it is around the history of my family, but other events are unexplained. Growing up in Brooklyn has taught me so much about life's expectations, joy, disappointment, people, and fear. I will attempt to explain them to you with the best of my recollection.

I am an ordinary person, who has experienced life from many perspectives. I have always been a lucky person, and many good things have happened to me. I have been very successful in business; my education is limited, and I have depended on hard work, good ethics, and always being extremely professional. I also learned in the business world that talking less is always better; let your client or competition do all the talking, while you take it all in. I've been blessed with a child, a daughter who has brought me so many memories, that it is impossible to think I can write them all down in a book. I have found love at the age of forty-five years, and I understand now what it is like to be in a relationship. There is a certain give and take that you need to work on, and the reason you work on it is because you want it to work, that you're in love and life is better with that person. I've learned that you don't need to please everybody, all the time; that sometimes, no matter how unpopular your choices are, you need to think of yourself. You need to have hope in your life, no matter how bleak the current situation is, you should always have hope. God should be in your life every day, because you need to be humbled and it's good to believe there is a superior being that can guide you through difficult times. How else can you deal with the passing of your father, to get the strength to hold him while he takes his last breath?

My life has been all of this and more.

Chapter 1

Dad in Shallow

It was October 6 and I was driving in my car to the cemetery. I was feeling a little down; I've been thinking about my dad a lot. I can't get myself to stop crying when I'm alone. My dad passed away on September 15, and it's very hard to believe he's not with us anymore. That is what is really making me depressed, the fact that I won't see him again in this world, that is. The traffic on Route 1 North is terrible; here I am at a standstill in my car and I can't stop crying.

I looked up from a seat in the back of the classroom. My brother Richie was sitting next to me. The classroom looked familiar, like an old movie of a time past. It was my junior high school, Shallow 226. My dad, brother, and I attended this school. We were always proud about being students at PS 226. My father was a star athlete in his time. There were photos up on the hallway walls of him winning track meets, swinging a baseball bat, and standing next to Mr. Ronaldson, the gym teacher. I glanced over to my brother, who gestured to the front of the class. There was a man wearing a shiny gray suit, the kind President Kennedy wore in the early sixties. The man was tall and lean; he was addressing the packed classroom. Everyone was looking straight at him, listening with such enthusiasm to every word he spoke. Richie pointed to a desk right up front and told me to go sit there. I got up and walked to the front of the class and sat down in the chair. All of a sudden, I looked up at the man speaking to the class, and I couldn't believe my eyes. He was so energetic; he had a smile from ear to ear. He seemed to be so happy, speaking and addressing the whole class. At that point, the man glanced over at me and suddenly stopped for a moment. I'm very happy to see you he said with a great big smile, "I'm glad you could make it," and then he continued to speak again to the class. I immediately turned around to see my brother; I wanted to know if he was seeing the same vision as me.

Richie has always been the cool one; nothing fazes him, and I guess that comes with the big territory. Back to the front of the classroom. He was so handsome, so young, and so full of life. The man speaking to the class was my father, a way I never seen him before, at least not in person. I've seen all the photos of him, of my mom dating him, getting married, with my brother and me, but never like this. I'm sure this is the man my mother fell in love with as a young woman in the fifties. Did he know I was his son, or was he just excited about what he was talking about? I looked back again towards Richie and mow I could tell he saw exactly what I saw, our dad, young, handsome, full of life, that unbelievable smile, throughout my life it would light up a room. Where am I? How did I get here? Can I talk to him? First of all, our father was a shoemaker by trade. The only public speaking I ever saw of him was when he was coaching a bunch of kids on a ball field.

My father finished his speech and the class let out. Richie and I, frozen in our seats, stared straight ahead at our dad. All of a sudden, he spoke to us. "Did you enjoy my lecture?" I couldn't speak a reply, I sat there, mouth open, staring.

"Yes, I'll never forget it," announced Richie from the back of the room as he jumped up from his seat.

"Oh yeah, is that so?" our dad replied. "What was so unforgettable, my son?"

"Well, sir," said my brother, "you remind me and my little brother of a man we know. Actually, he is a great man to be more accurate, a man that has taught us so much about life, love, and most important, family."

Our dad was taken aback a bit. He stared curiously at my brother and me. He looked at me almost as if he knew me. I was thinking, could it be I resemble someone he knows, maybe himself at my age? My brother looks more like my mom, and I have the lighter coloring and look of my dad. Our dad had to be about twenty-four years old, standing in front of us at this moment.

"Well, I'll tell you what we're going to do. Why don't you boys come up here and help me pack up my belongings and maybe I can hear a little bit about this great man you speak of." Richie and I helped pack up our dad's papers. Actually, I did nothing but stare at him. He must've thought I was slow or been hit in the head with a baseball.

Richie and I left the classroom with our young dad and continued out of the school. Now nothing of the school looked familiar to me, but nevertheless it was still our junior high school. We spent a full afternoon with our dad. He took us to the candy store on 66th Street and New Utrecht Avenue. This store has been closed since 1980, the owner long retired and living in Florida. The last time I was in this candy store was 1972. I went into the candy store with a bunch of my friends and ordered an egg cream. Out of all my friends in the store, the man looked at me and instantly knew my last name was Prestipino. Now it almost makes sense; we've met before. Here I was sitting next to my dad and brother while the owner chatted with our dad about the New York Giants baseball team. The neighborhood looked different; the store looked so modern and clean. I like it a lot. The cars outside were all antique cars in perfect condition. As the afternoon went on, we told our dad about our dad. What a great baseball player he was, coach, father, teacher, husband, and son. We told him stories that were very similar to his real life. He would just shake his head and say, "You don't say." We told him how beautiful and intelligent our mother was. He seemed to be very interested to hear our opinion of our mother. We told him our mom had a strong personality. She was tall, slim, with beautiful dark skin, big black eyes, and jet-black hair, just like Richie. "So you must look like your father," our dad said to me.

I swallowed a bit and said, "People say I do." Our dad began to talk about his family, his two sisters, Vinnie and Marie. Marie was the baby; we knew that already, and almost slipped when he was talking. At one point, two of my father's best friends walked in, Red and Beef. We knew them as Uncle Red and Uncle Beef. They were very polite and friendly to us. Uncle Red and Uncle Beef were my dad's best friends, and they stayed that way until they both passed away in the '90s. I'm not sure how we got here, but I'm enjoying myself tremendously. I've been in similar situations before, but not many with my brother. All I can remember at this moment is that I was driving to the cemetery, it was October 2004, and he was nearly gone from our life a month. Our dad had such a positive impact in our life that we were all having problems dealing with his passing. Back at the candy store, it started to get dark outside, and for some reason, our dad didn't seem too surprised that we spent the entire afternoon together talking, listening to his stories, talking about his life, telling us what he wanted to accomplish during his lifetime, the legacy he would love to leave behind someday, knowing that he made a difference in someone's life. From what our dad was saying, he wasn't dating anyone at this time, but also was not in a hurry to get married. There was a reason Richie and I came here and met our dad ten years before he had his first son. If only he knew at that moment how his two sons admired, loved, and respected him. I'm not sure why this chance meeting happen, but for some reason our dad always led by example, said and did the right things. Did he guide us through life or did we guide him? My guess is we were meant to be a family, and family always helps each other through difficult times with no questions asked.

The year was 1940-something and 2004

Mom, Richie, Dad and me

Me Princess and Richie

Chapter 2

Life on the Bowery

New York City is an unbelievable place to live, and even greater to visit. I can honestly say there is not a city in the world that compares to it. Just about every city in the United States wants to emulate New York. They can only hope to generate the revenues and tourism that exist in New York City. Entertainment, sports, theater is at the highest level. The New York Yankees are the most popular baseball team in the world. If you did a survey in any other city or country and asked what baseball team you would want to see play, just about everyone would say the New York Yankees. Let's face it, when the Yankees are not in the World Series, viewing ratings are way down. I know for a fact I don't watch the World Series when the Yankees are not in it, but maybe that's just a New Yorker talking. I lived a short time in Manhattan when I was going through my divorce; living in New York was one of the greatest experiences I ever had. You may think for the obvious reason, but not so. I enjoyed walking to the gym, shopping in the local grocery store, recognizing my neighbors in the street, and sometimes just staring out the window of my eighteenth-floor apartment. I could hear the cars passing my building on FDR Drive. I could almost tell what time of day it was by the seconds delay between passing cars. My apartment was on 37th Street and First Avenue. The building was named Manhattan Place Condos; it had a doorman, fitness center on the top floor, and a great pool for doing laps, which was located in an all-year-round atrium with great views of Manhattan.

I just got off the phone with Janet; she was getting ready to leave her apartment in New Jersey and would drive into the City to meet me. She would park her car under the building for the day. We had a busy day planned; we're going to Orchard Street near Delancey and Bowery Street. I was looking to buy a leather coat and do some shopping. Afterwards, we plan to have lunch in SoHo; Janet has a few favorite restaurants in the area and prefers to do her shopping there as well. I figured I had some time before Janet arrived at my apartment; it was a beautiful morning, so I decided to go out for a walk. I threw on a sweater and walked out of my apartment to the elevators. Manhattan Place Condos had three elevators, one slower than the others; you could wait a good five minutes before an elevator would come for you. I got on the elevator and there was an elderly couple already on the elevator car. I walked in and said good morning.

I was outside on the street; the street was busy, people were all over the place, and the sidewalks were filled with people rushing in both directions. Cars were at a standstill and the noise of the car motors was louder than I ever heard before. The year, I would venture to guess, was 1919, and I was standing on the corner of Bowery and Delancey in the middle of the day. I had no idea why I was here or how long I was going to stay. No way to call Janet and tell her I may be a little late; actually, I'm just kidding about that, but thought it anyway. I looked at my reflection in a store window and noticed that I look about the same age I look in the year 2001; my hair is short, my build is slim, and I feel about the same age, if that makes any sense at all. It's a mild and sunny day on the Bowery; I really don't know what to do. I guess I'll take a walk, maybe I can get something to eat. There are delicatessens, meat markets, vegetable stands, fish markets, and vendors all along the street. I was standing in front of a residential building; in 2001, this building will be called pre-war buildings. Five-story apartments with no elevator. The apartments are big and are capable of housing an entire family. Off to where I was standing, I can see a young family, a young woman who looks too young to be the mother, maybe she's the older sister, two boys and a girl huddled next to each other. The sight of this young family worries me; for some reason, I have an immediate connection to them, some weird force that is pulling me to them. I can sense sadness, sorrow, uncertainty, and fear of the unknown. The young woman doesn't look like she belongs here on the Bowery among the hustle and bustle of this typical New York scene. The young woman is now talking to a man in his forties. The man looks as though he is of Italian descent, he has a slick, not-so-trustworthy look, and he is dressed in a brown tweed suit with fine pinstripes. He looks very sharp and out of place down here. The young woman is clearly upset and is having a hard time understanding and dealing with this man. I have no idea what is taking place, but feel obligated to interfere. I walk over to get a little closer to this family, so I can hear what is being said. The man is telling the young woman, "Don't worry, I'll take good care of your boy, I will personally watch over him and in return, your family will have a place to stay, and you will have the opportunity to work to pay your rent in this apartment."

At this point, I don't know why I did it, but I felt I had to intervene, Normally in the world I'm from, I would never get involved. I let people work their own problems out, but I decided to walk right up to the young lady and introduce myself. "Hello, thank God, you made it here safe and sound. I've missed you so much."

Immediately, the man looked at me and was taken aback a bit. "Who are you? Who are you?" he asked again.

"Never mind who I am. Before you decide the fate of my niece and nephews, you will have to talk to me." The young woman, who is now in total shock and is speechless, is staring up at me and can't speak a word. Can you imagine this young girl in a strange city now has two smooth-talking men to deal with? Lucky for Grace, I was one of the men; she would have nothing to worry about from me. I pulled this man to the side, and within minutes, I uncovered he was a fraud, a con man, looking to make a quick dollar with this young woman and her kids or siblings. Even though we were the same age, I could tell I was physically in far superior shape than this man. Don't forget, in 1919, men didn't exercise, lift weights, ride a bike, or jog, especially a con man, who smoked and drank, I would assume. I grabbed him by his coat collars and leaned into him to force him against the wall of the building. I was pleasantly surprised to see how easily I could manhandle this person. I whispered into his ear, "What is your name and what is your business here?" He said it was none of my business and I didn't know who I was speaking to. I started thinking, or should I say I hoped I wouldn't be around much longer to see if I made a mistake. I put one hand on his Adam's apple and the other into his pocket; I reached into his pocket and pulled out a wad of bills and a pocket watch. I quickly slipped it into my pocket. I warned this man that if I hear that he approaches or talks to this family or involves them in anything, I will come back personally to speak to him. I knew I was going home eventually, so I told him my name, or should I say half my name. "My name is Frank Prestipino, I'm from Cefalu, Sicily, and I am personally responsible for this family." Of course, my real name is Gary Frank Prestipino, but I didn't think Gary was going to intimidate this person as much as Frank Prestipino would. I didn't realize how tight my hand was around this man's neck; he started getting a little faint on me. I could tell his legs were giving way, so I released my hold on him and pushed him to the sidewalk. "Now get up and walk away as fast as you can. I don't ever want to see you in this neighborhood again." He wobbled to his feet and to my surprise, without a word or whimper, limped away. I have to say my heart was beating 1,000 beats a minute, but it felt great. I'm not much of an intimidating person in the year 2001, but it seemed I had a slight advantage in 1919.

I walked over to the young woman, who was just standing on the sidewalk with her arms around her three children. Yes, she was the young widow mother of these three young children. I introduce myself and apologize for my bullish behavior. "My name is Frank Prestipino, pleased to meet you. I'm very sorry if I startled you, but that man had bad intentions for you and your family. My name is Grace Palame, this is…"

I interrupted her immediately. "Did you say Grace Palame?"

The woman said, "Yes; no, I mean yes, my name is Grace Palame. My family and I are from Scranton, Pennsylvania." I looked over at the two boys and girl. They looked so scared and alone. They were dressed very nicely for this part of town. They probably lived a comfortable life in Scranton at one time.

"Let me guess, your names are? Let me see." I looked at the youngest child, a boy. I said, "I would think your name is John, is that correct?"

The oldest boy spoke. "How did you know that, sir?"

"Ah, Vincent, or shall I say James." I turned to look at the girl. "And you must be Nancy?"

At this point, Grace Palame had a bigger look of fear on her face as she did when the con man was talking to her. I apologize Mrs. Palame; I was standing over there and heard your children and you talking, you mentioned their names in conversation. One thing I can tell you is that man will not be bothering you any time soon.

I am talking to my great-grandma, Grandma Grace; she is not quite twenty-eight years old, widowed with three children just arrived in New York City. Here in front of me stand her three young children: Vincent my grandfather, John my great uncle, and Nancy my great aunt. My grandfather always talked about his childhood moving from Scranton to New York City on the Bowery. What should I say? What should I do? Maybe I should just say good day and let them go off on their own; remember, they adjusted just fine when I wasn't around.

"You need to find a safe, clean apartment for you and your family. Do you have any family in New York?"

Grace answered, "Not yet, but I have written my brother Jim (Jimanu as my grandfather called him) and he is on his way to New York with my mother. We have selected the Bowery to be our meeting place."

I replied, "Perfect, let's get you situated in the right apartment so you can wait for your brother and mother to come join you. First let's get some food into your children's stomachs and then we'll find an apartment." We walked down the street to a Jewish delicatessen. We ordered pastrami and knishes for all of us. I have to say I've never had knishes as good as the one I ate that day. I reached into my pocket and pulled out almost $95. I was surprised to see how money that man was carrying around on him. That just confirms that he was involved in some shady business. I paid the bill, left a five-cent tip, and off we went to look for a place to live. Down the street a bit, I saw there was a sign in the first-floor window: apartment for let. Grace, me, and the kids went inside. After haggling a bit with the landlord, and assuring him I would always be around to pay the rent and look after my nieces and nephews, we all agreed on the price and the terms. Eight dollars a month rent paid up in advance and one month's security. I was starting to feel uncomfortable being around my great-grandma and grandfather. My grandfather Jim was my favorite person when I was growing up. More than half of my experiences were because of this man. Now here he is, a young boy no more than nine years old. I can see the sadness in his eye; he missed his father so much. I knew that already, though. I knew from all the conversations we had when I was growing up. How he respected and loved his dad so much, even as a grownup and as a grandfather when he talked about his father, tears would come to his eyes. I couldn't imagine life without my father; what an emptiness I would've experienced without him. I knew my time here was coming to an end; I started feeling faint and disoriented. I paid the rent for six months, plus a month's deposit, $56 to the landlord. I gave Grace the rest of the money I had left in my pocket. Of course she didn't want to take it. I explained that I would never see her again and that she had to be strong and she was on her own. I asked her if I could have a word with her oldest son, James. She welcomed it; she knew her son was hurting, and that he had gone through so much when his father was dying. Maybe a talk with an older, wiser man would help him, I knew it too, my grandfather would talk about his dad and how he tried to help him, but the doctors couldn't save him anyway. It hurt him as much when he was an adult.

"James, you're going to have a great life. You're going to make a difference in a lot of people's lives," I explained. "I want to tell you more, but I can't at this moment. It's not always fair, but you're the man of your family, you have to take care of your mom, brother, and sister." At that moment, I reached back into my pocket and pulled out the gold pocket watch I had lifted from the con man, I know it wasn't right taking the watch, it was too late I can't give it back. "Here, take this watch, think of the future, think of me, think of your family."

James smiled at me. I know that smile; I've seen it all my life. "Thank you, sir, thank you. I will never forget you; my family will never forget you." James gave me a hug.

"Have a good day," I replied.

The elderly couple walking out of the elevator were saying goodbye to me. "Oh yes, thank you, you too."

My hands in my pocket, I pulled out my grandfather's pocket watch to see what time it was — 9:35. About four minutes had passed since I got on the elevator and traveled from 2001 back to 1919 and back. Yes, my grandfather gave me that pocket watch years later when I was a young adult. He would always say he knew who the pocket watch belonged to and that there was only one person he would ever give the pocket watch to. In all the years, he never said that person was me, but one day when he knew he was getting on in years and his health was rapidly declining he may've thought his time on earth was nearing an end, he decided to give me the watch. He sat me down in the rose garden in the back yard of his house. His words were very familiar. He told me, "I will never forget you, this is your watch. Take it and remember: think of the future, think of me, and think of your family."

We both smile and hug each other.

The year November 2001 and fall 1919

Grandpa Jim is standing behind grandma Grace
Aunt Nancy and Uncle John beside grandma

Chapter 3

Yankees 3 Detroit 2 what a night

It was August 1969. I was eleven years old, and baseball was the most important thing in my life. I was a big Yankees fan during the downslide period of the Yankee organization. George Steinbrenner was still about five or six years away from buying the Yankees and changing the organization forever. The Yankees didn't win many games in 1969, but that didn't matter much to me. I loved watching games and I loved rooting for my favorite player. Bobby Murcer was a young up–and-coming star on a team with mediocre talent. The first time I saw Bobby Murcer playing, he was at shortstop. A ground ball was rocked toward him. Bobby cleanly picked up the ball and tossed it over the first baseman's head and twenty rows into the first base stands. I decided right than and there that Bobby Murcer was going to be my hero. Of course, Bobby didn't stay at shortstop too long. Bobby could hit; he had the Yankee Stadium lefty swing that provided many exciting home runs. For years, Bobby produced great numbers, average, and home runs.

Bobby was supposed to be the next Mickey Mantle. I saw Mantle toward the end of his career and didn't quite understand the attention. Of course, I know now that Mickey Mantle is probably on the top ten list of all-time greatest baseball players ever. Nevertheless, Bobby was my guy. I had posters, magazines, and collected cards of him.

When I was a kid growing up in New York, I listened to most of the games on the radio. Believe it or not, even in 1969, most baseball games were not televised. In fact, they were in black-and-white. The Yankees were on WPIX, channel 11, Getty was the big sponsor; every commercial was for Getty Gas. The Mets were on WOR, channel 9. I truly believe I learned baseball because of two things. My dad was the most knowledgeable person on baseball. He was born to be a coach; he could see flaws in your swing or motion that if corrected properly, would change you from an average player to an above-average player. My dad was, for his time, way ahead of the professional brain trust that managed Major League Baseball. He taught my brother and me the basics skills of baseball. Throwing overhand, running on your toes, how to slide, hook slide included, and how to hit. My stance at the plate turns out to be about thirty years ahead of the major league players today. Most batters in the '70s held their bat high and back, ready to uncork a powerful swing. My stance was relaxed, with the bat up and in the middle of my body, not till the pitcher was ready to go into his wind-up and deliver the pitch did I cock my bat back and up and stepping into to every pitch. I was a righty because my brother and father were righty hitters. My dad saw right away I was not a natural righty hitter, but rather a natural lefty swinger. He taught me how to drive the ball to left and right center, the downward swing that is so popular today with players such as Derek Jeter and Alex Rodriguez. I won't get into too many details at this moment about my baseball skills. I think baseball is the only time in my life I let my father down. This was when I was in high school. All I'll say at this time is that my brother and I had the skills and inherited talent of our dad to take the sport to the next level. It was a big disappointment to my dad. Now as an adult and father, I realized I could've provided my dad a dream-come-true life. Don't take it wrong, it's not something my dad ever harped on, but after all our years together, I know if my brother Richie or I had become a professional major league ball player, his life would've been complete. My dad himself was a great athlete; he was a track and field star, and he ran the 100-yard dash in nine-something seconds, for his era that was unbelievable.

He was an amazing shortstop with such finesse and style, who could hit a ninety-mile-an-hour fastball from both sides of the plate, and when you weren't on your toes would steal home at will. Whenever I start talking about baseball, my dad comes to mind, I get off on a tangent. I can actually see him playing ball as a young man. Later on in my book, I will tell stories of times I traveled back in time and played side-by-side with the greatest baseball player ever.

My short story is about one particular night at Yankee Stadium with my father. It was late in the season. I'm sure the Yankees were not mathematically eliminated from winning the pennant, but with no chance of ever winning it. It was a night game; the weather was overcast with light rain all day and into the night. My dad and I had tickets and we were going to the game no matter what the weather was. In those days, we would get to the stadium hours before the game started. Batting and fielding practice was almost better than the game itself. Just watching the ball players work on their hitting skills in the cages, the infield drills, pepper games, coaches hitting flies to the outfielders with a fungo bat was a thrill in itself.

I had a broken arm and full cast up to my shoulder and had it resting in a sling.

As soon as we got to the stadium, I ran down to the field level and was leaning on to the field. Detroit took the field and started their fielding practice. Then the Yankees came out to the field and began their warm-up drills. Throughout the practice, I was trying to get Bobby Murcer's attention. I was looking for Bobby to sign my cast or just say hi. I caught Bobby's attention and he gestured over to me that he would come over in a minute. I immediately looked back to my dad and he gave me a smile of encouragement. Within minutes, the rain began to fall heavier and my dad called for me to come back under cover. So I retreated back up under the mezzanine section till the rain stopped. The remainder of batting practice was cancelled and the ball players went back to the locker rooms.

The game was slightly delayed to give time to get the field ready. The rain was still falling as a steady drizzle. As the players were announced, I noticed my hero, Bobby Murcer, was not in the lineup that night. I remember being so disappointed that I wasn't going to see Bobby Murcer play this night. My dad and I had great seats for this game. We were sitting on the first-base side of the stadium, fifteen to twenty rows from the dugout. Because of the rain, we actually moved back further to get under cover from the rain. The game was a pitchers' duel. I'm not sure who pitched for either team. If I'm not mistaken, it may've been Denny McClain for Detroit. He was a great pitcher who one year won thirty games for Detroit. The night was cold and damp, but my dad and I refused to leave before the last out. Going out to the ball park to see my baseball team and favorite player play baseball was great, but I have to tell you with no exaggeration, just sitting right next to my father in the stadium, listening to him talk baseball was all I ever really cared about.

It was the ninth inning, the Yankees were losing two to zero, the rain and wind were picking up a little bit more, but we hung in there; no way we were leaving. The Yankees managed to get two runners on base after two quick outs in the bottom of the ninth inning. All of a sudden, the house speaker or announcer announced that Bobby Murcer is now coming to plate to pinch hit. I can't tell you who he was pinch hitting for, or who was pitching for Detroit. As soon as Bobby was announced, the Detroit manager came out to the mound and brought in a lefty reliever.

All of a sudden, the park was filled with excitement; the fans began to make noise. The relief pitcher took his warm-ups, and Bobby came back out of the dugout and walked very confidently to the batter's box. I looked at my dad, and he at me. "Son," my dad said, "look at your hero. He knows he has three swings to make a difference."

The relief pitcher winds up and delivers his first pitch towards home plate, Bobby swings and crushes the ball into the right field stands. A three-run pinch-hit game-winning home run in the bottom of the ninth with two outs, down two runs to nothing. Bobby Murcer, with one swing of the bat, made one rainy summer night at Yankee Stadium a memory that would last my entire life.

My dad and I would always talk about this night and the drama of the ending of the game. The game meant nothing to the Yankees pennant chances, I will always remember this game, as my baseball hero Bobby Murcer hit the game-winning home run, and my everyday hero, my dad, who worked all day in a factory, came home from work, changed, had a quick bite to eat, took the train from Brooklyn to the Bronx, stood in the rain till the very end of a game that had no real meaning, just so his boy could watch the Yankees beat the Detroit Tigers 3 to 2 in the ninth inning.

My dad and I walked out onto the field after the game to visit the monuments in center field.

What a night!

Thanks, Dad!

Chapter 4

Slide home

Baseball is the greatest sport ever; there is no other sport in the world that has a much history as baseball. There are more legends, heroes, and interesting personalities in baseball than any other sport. I loved playing baseball growing up as a kid in Brooklyn; I played as often as I could, from morning to night, and some days into the dark. My friends and I would organize games against other neighborhoods; these games were fiercely played, and the rivalries between the neighborhoods were intense. I can remember many of the games ended in fights and arguments over a close call or a hard slide into a base. My dad would talk baseball to my brother and me all the time. We heard stories of all the great ones and of some of the greatest games ever played. My dad was a New York Giants fan during his days. He played some semi-pro baseball and also played for the equivalent of the basketball Harlem Globetrotters, the Kokomo Clowns. I also played organized baseball for some traveling leagues. The ball players' skills and competition were at the highest level imaginable for sandlot ball. It's not like it is today, when you have to worry about some kid's feelings, and no matter what, you have to play a kid for at least one or two innings. They didn't have tee ball when I started playing. My first year playing Little League, I didn't make contact with the ball the entire season. There wasn't some kid's father pitching the ball to me over the plate so I could hit it. There was a kid the same age as me, throwing strikes, balls, and bean balls at times. Some kids peak sooner than others; at the end of your childhood career, you either catch up, pass the early peakers, or you already quit playing baseball, because you just don't have it. If a seven-year-old kid had a first season like the one I had in 1964, his parents would've brought him to a psychologist, or bought him a flat-screen TV. The parents, the coach, and the whole league would've known about it. The funny part about my first year playing Little League, I remember it so clearly, I could remember a lot of games; I remember a ground ball bouncing off my chest or just plain going through my legs, swinging at a pitch a foot over my head and seeing the third base coach cringe. Oh yeah, that's not supposed to happen today either. Could you imagine pulling a seven-year-old kid off the field in the middle of the inning? What I'm trying to say is I do not have one bad memory of that first season; I enjoyed every moment of it. In fact, when I finally got a base hit my second year, it felt so good. I think my mom and Dad took me to Spumoni Gardens for Italian ices. My father was the greatest coach ever; he coached my brother Richie's teams more than mine because Richie was the oldest, so my dad started coaching Richie early. Richie reached his peak early and was professional material when he stopped playing. Thank God my dad coached Richie; he broke every rule of today's coaching guide on my brother. He yelled at him from practice through the game. He hit infield grounders the hardest to my brother, and when they gave out the MVP at the end of the year to the most valuable player on the team, he gave it to another kid. Hands down, my brother was the MVP every year. Not once did he ever complain or cry to our mom. Even now, we always love to joke to our dad. My dad was a lot easier on me; maybe he knew I would react better to calmness. Again, I didn't mature to the level my brother was until my first year in high school.

This is where my story actually begins. I was playing baseball for the varsity team of Franklin Delano Roosevelt High School in Brooklyn, New York. I was a freshman and I tried out for the varsity squad, but neglected to tell the coach I wasn't a sophomore. When I made the team and had to show my report card to the coach, he almost flipped. He had me playing second base and batting third. We were in the best baseball division in all of New York; we had powerhouse teams such as Lafayette, New Utrecht, Lincoln, and Ft. Hamilton. When I was playing high school baseball, Lafayette won the division all four years. I had friends and teammates from my traveling team who were great baseball players and sat on the bench at Lafayette. When my dad was in high school, he was a star baseball player for New Utrecht High School. They won the championship every year he was there.

Mr. Mascara, the coach, rearranged my schedule so I could get out earlier enough to play in the afternoon games. Freshmen in FDR went to school from 10:30 AM to 4:30 PM. Because of the number of kids attending the school, they would spilt the schedules with sophomores.

FDR's rival was New Utrecht, mainly because the two teams were fairly matched. We would play each team three times during the regular season, and all three games were played in the same week, Monday, Wednesday, and Friday. Unfortunately for FDR, all our games against New Utrecht were played on their field, in front of all their fans. FDR didn't have a home field; we would play some of our home games at Aramus Field when Aramus wasn't using it.

This one particular game, I was having a good day at the plate. New Utrecht had this hard-throwing lefty pitching. I think his name was Danny Murphy. I played against him in travel ball as well. He had a big sweeping motion and came in a little sidearm when facing lefty hitters such as me. I had this stubborn attitude when facing him that I was not going to give an inch in the box, and would take him to center or left center every at-bat. If he was smart enough, all he had to do is put one of his eighty-plus-mile-an hour fastballs inside on me and he would have cut me in half. I guess I out-intimidated him. He probably didn't want to hit or hurt me, so he put his fast ball down the middle or on the outside of the plate. I would just wait and smack it to center or left center, usually for an extra-base hit. I had good speed, and if I hit a ball in the gap, I could stretch it into a double or triple fairly easily. My third time up in the game, I hit a line drive down the left field line and got a stand-up triple. When I arrived at third base, my coach was screaming at me because he had given me the bunt sign. He wanted me to drag a bunt single down the first base line. I saw the sign, but thought, he must be mistaken, I hit this guy hard every time I face him. So I just swung away and ended up on third base. While he was ranting on about being a team player and that he was going to bench me for the rest of the week, I started to feel a little weird, I was feeling a little out of my surroundings, I couldn't explain it, though. I looked around and I was still standing on third base. I was still at New Utrecht High School baseball field. Then it hit me; I looked down at my uniform. It was a lot baggier and heavier, the cotton material was not like the polyester uniform I was wearing. I'm wearing a New Utrecht baseball uniform now, I'm standing on third base, and the coach is telling me to pay attention to his signs. The field looks so much different from what I'm used to, but overall, it just looks like an older version of a baseball field. You know, not much grass and plenty of dirt. I've been here before, I know I have; I can't figure out in my mind what I'm doing here and why, but I know exactly what I'm supposed to do. Again the third base coach is telling me, "Stay on your toes, there's two outs, remember, go on anything hit." I notice the pitcher is in a full windup delivering to the plate, he has a high kick and slow overhand motion. Most pitchers today do not use the high kick or over-the-top motion. I lead off third for the first pitch; it was a high-and-inside ball one. The pitcher is taking a little longer than usual between the next pitch, eventually he winds and delivers strike one. All of a sudden, I know what I have to do. I can still hear the coach giving instructions: "Go on a hit ball or passed ball." The pitcher begins his slow delivery, and I take off towards home. My head is down and I am running faster than I could imagine I could run. I know I'm pretty fast, but I never felt myself run this fast before. It seemed like I was running an inch or two off the ground. I can start to hear people yelling "he's going, he's going" and a lot of other people just cheering. With a flash, I was about ten feet from home plate; the ball was on its way to the plate. The catcher stood up from his crouch position in anticipation of me sliding into home. As I approach home plate, the right-handed batter in the box begins his swings. I throw my legs from under me and slide feet-first into home plate. My hands in the air and the batter swinging inches over my head, I reach home plate before the ball lands in the catcher's mitt and the batter misses strike two.

"Safe, safe!" yelled the home plate umpire as I jumped up and ran towards the dugout like nothing big had happened at all. My teammates all gathered around me, patting me on the back and congratulating me. I just stole home, I slid under a swinging hitter and into home plate, I just traveled back or jumped back to 1939, into the uniform and shoes that were worn by my dad, Natale Prestipino. I heard this story many times over the years from his friends, and I actually saw a photo of it at my uncle Beef's house one day. A photographer for the *Chief,* a Brooklyn newspaper, happened to be at the game that day and he was alert enough to capture the slide into home plate.

"Do you understand what I'm saying? Do you understand me? Look at me, I said." Mr. Mascara is screaming at me again. Maybe I zone out and travel to another time. Nevertheless, Mr. Mascara seems to still be upset with my triple. As I always did, I smile and ignore him, which made him even more furious. I have this way of listening to someone and giving them the impression I understand completely what they mean, and that I will do exactly what they want me to do, but the end result is me doing exactly what I want. I know this trait of mine sometimes drives my wife Janet crazy.

Hearing Mr. Mascara screaming, I realize I'm back in 1973, standing on third base in the New Utrecht High School baseball field, wearing my 100% polyester FDR baseball uniform. I look over to the coach still screaming at me. I yelled back at him **"YES I UNDERSTAND, I UNDERSTAND YOU PERFECTLY!!!!"** I looked away from my coach and glanced over at the pitcher, I noticed he was standing on the mound ready to pitch, but he wasn't in the stretch position anymore, but going into a full windup. I began creeping off third base and my lead was getting further away from the bag than usual. I could hear Mr. Mascara in a loud whisper, saying "get back, get back." As soon as the pitcher turns his eyes towards home plate, I took off to towards home. My head down, my cleats digging up dirt as I ran as fast as I could. The scene was oh so familiar to me now, the coach screaming in the background, the players yelling **"HE'S GOING, HE'S GOING,"** the crowd cheering. Wait!! There was something wrong; there was something different. It didn't feel exactly the same. In a split second, I figured it out: My feet were digging into the dirt and throwing dirt as they always do when I run, they weren't an inch or two off the ground as I dashed towards home plate, I didn't feel like I was running on air the way they had felt when I was in my dad's uniform. Either way, I approached home plate within seconds. The pitcher delivered a perfect strike right down the middle of the plate. The batter standing in the right hander batter's box saw me out of the corner of his eye; he immediately stepped out of the box. Someone should teach him how to play baseball for sure. The catcher stood up and stepped up to meet the pitch and me. As I did just a few moments ago, or should I say forty years ago, I threw my legs from under me and I slid hard into home plate . **"YOU'RE OUT!"** the umpire shouted.

Oh boy, I'm in big trouble!!

My dad and his high school team

Chapter 5

The journey from boy to man

One of my earliest stories of my grandfather's life

The year was November 1918 in the coal mine town of Scranton, Pennsylvania. Winter came early that year. My grandfather remembered it vividly, it was unusually cold for this time of year. Why a nine-year-old boy would take notice is strange in itself. Snow had already fallen and the ground was covered with a white blanket of snow. My grandfather would always say when it snowed, he would think of this particular point in his life. James, my grandfather, who was that nine- year-old boy in 1918, tells me the story of the day he grew up faster than he or anyone else had planned for him. My grandfather loved living in Scranton; his parents had a modest home and were living well for the times. James had a younger sister and brother, Nancy and John. I always loved being around Aunt Nancy and Uncle John; they were such good people. They treated my brother Richie and me so well. James's mother Grace was a very young mother; she gave birth to James when she was fifteen years old. James's dad, Salvatore Palame, was an Italian immigrant from Sicily, who came to the United States in 1907 with his young bride Grace Alba from Palermo, Sicily. Grace Alba was a beautiful woman; her ethnic European features, her young, innocent Italian olive color made her stand out like the Statue of Liberty in the New York Harbor. When Grace walked down the streets of this small coal mine town, people took notice. Her body straight as board, head held high, looking straight ahead and into the eyes of every townsperson she encountered. This was a woman who was so confident and secure, she was living in a town, not knowing the language, and many miles away from her small village in Sicily. She was a child herself. My grandfather would tell me the story how his father proposed to his mother's father. The way it went, according to my grandfather, was something like this: His father had some land that he grew olives on, a few cows that produced milk, and a promise to take care of his oldest daughter and to take her to a new and promising world (America). In Scranton, James's father worked in the coal mines, like every other man in the town. It was a difficult life — hard work, long hours, terrible working conditions, but it provided a modest home for his family and put food on the table. After a few years of working deep in the coal mines, James's father became ill, he contracted lung disease, something in that era they called black lung disease or coal miner's disease. James's father worked as long as he could, until it wasn't possible anymore to lift himself out of bed and go to the mine and work a ten-hour day. My grandfather's dad was a big man; he stood six feet four inches tall and had striking looks, long dark hair that flopped about his head and in front of his eyes at times. Life was good in Scranton; my grandfather was getting a good education and his family lived well. James's father was getting worse by the day; it seemed that the doctor would stop by the house in the morning and also in the evening on his way home.

James was sitting in the living room on a chilly November night, reading, when suddenly his mom came into the room and instructed James to get dressed, that he had to journey three miles in the dark through the forest, to the outskirts of the town, to Doctor Allman's home office. His mom said to tell the doctor that his father was very sick and he needed to come right away. James never hesitated; he slipped on his shoes and ran out of the house, straight towards the dark, thick woods. As James ran out on the front porch, he stopped and looked up at the dark blue sky; he noticed there was an almost-full moon. To his relief, this would provide enough light to guide him through the dark forest. Many leaves had already fallen off of the trees and were mixed with fallen snow and rain from the previous day's snowfall.

Years later, when I was a child, my grandfather would say it was the most frightening experience of his life. He couldn't remember if he was shaking from the cold or from fear.

James took off through the woods, running through the thick, cold, wet leaves, his eyes darting all around him, his heart beating so fast and loud, it felt like it was going to explode out of his chest. James had a fear of the woods, the wild dogs, snakes, and every other wild animal his imagination could think of. As James sprinted through the woods, all he could see in his mind was the look on his mother's face, the seriousness in her voice, the fear in her eyes. She didn't resemble that young girl that his sister, brother, and he called Mama. Years later, he realized it was the look of a woman who knew her life was changing forever. It seemed like he was running for hours, when all of sudden, James's feet went from under him and he began to drop out of thin air. Down he slid, and it seemed like he slid thirty feet straight down an embankment. He tried to grab branches or anything he could reach, his arms flapping wildly. When he came to a stop, he was completely wet and covered with mud, snow, and leaves. He shook himself off, looked around, spotted the moon behind him, and proceeded to run away from it like it was chasing him. No sooner did James pick up speed, but two wild dogs appeared within five feet of him. His biggest fear during normal circumstances was dogs, all dogs, big ones, small ones, it didn't matter much to him, just that he didn't like these four-legged animals. But now, standing in the middle of the forest in the cold dark of the night were these two wolflike animals, staring straight into his eyes. James could hear in the background a slight noise; it sounded like leaves blowing, or the wind against the trees or maybe water, a running stream or river. James, without another thought, started to run to the noise. At first the dogs didn't move, but suddenly, like a signal to attack, they began to chase after their prey. James could sense the natural instinct to attack their prey and determination in the wolf dogs, and knew he had to reach the water quickly. Why or how did he know the dogs would not follow him into the ice-cold water? Just a guess, a prayer or hope for himself. By the time James reached the ice water, all fear had escaped his body. He no longer was scared of the wild dogs or the dark forest. At that moment in time, James was being transformed into the man of the family, the one single person that a family has, the person everyone will count on to protect and make things right, the most important person in the family, the man of the family. James knew that he had to continue, the look on his mother's face still etched in his mind. James knew the family needed his help. James pushed himself harder. He ran through the ice-cold running brook across to the other side, never slowing down to notice how cold his legs were and how frostbitten his feet were. James didn't bother to take notice that the wild dogs had not attempted to cross the freezing water, and gave up their pursuit of attacking him. James could see a dim light coming from the distance. The light was becoming brighter quickly. He was running so fast that he shot out of the woods like a cannonball being fired from a cannon. Never did he slow down, even when he noticed he was in a wide open field approaching Doctor Allman's small country home. James quickly ran up to the front porch of Doctor Allman's home, and started knocking on the door. It was a few minutes before the doctor opened the front door; it seemed like eternity to James. As the doctor opened the door, James thought to himself what do I say, do I say my dad is very sick, he's dying, or my mama said for you to come quickly? For a half a second, he froze, but then shouted out, "My name is Vincent Palame, I mean James Palame, and my mama said you have to come quickly to our home."

Doctor Allman understood immediately. His response was "You're Mr. Palame's oldest boy, James. Hurry up and run back around to the barn. I'll need you to help attach the horse to my wagon."

James didn't hesitate. He turned around and ran right to the back where the barn was. In the barn were three horses. The first one he came upon was short, odd-looking horse; it looked like it was out to pasture and didn't have a lot of speed in it. The next stall was a beautiful palomino with a blanket on her back; the palomino looked young and fast and ready to go. The third stall was a tall, lean, black horse; he looked anxious and nervous. James didn't know which one the doctor would use. James hoped it would be the fastest of the three, and hoped it wasn't the tall, lean black one. Moments later, the doctor ran into the stall with his bag in hand. "Quick," he said, "open Coal's stall and bring him out to cross ties."

He looked up at the three stalls and noticed the names on each stall. Black as Coal was the plate on the third stall. James hesitated for a moment, but forced himself to move forward into the stall. As he opened the stall, Coal seemed to step back and allow James to enter, almost to reassure him everything was going to be ok.

James grabbed the reins off the hook and as if on cue, Black as Coal bent his head down and allowed him to slip the rein and bit into his mouth and around his head. As soon as the bit was in Coal's mouth, he stood up straight and was ready to be led out of the stall. James backed Coal in between the two poles coming from the wagon. Coal was cool as can be, and he allowed my grandfather to strap him into the harness. Doctor Allman yelled for James to open the barn doors. He pushed the two swinging doors wide open, and without hesitation, the doctor took off through the open barn doors into the cold night. He yelled back at James to check the horses and lock up the barn. James just stood there motionless, looking out at the fading image of Black as Coal and Doctor Allman pulling away from the barn. he dropped down to his needs and cried. James eventually checked the horses; he didn't know why, but he filled water buckets and put a blanket around the short old mare whose name was Rusty. He felt a certain connection to the horses in the stall in this very old barn. James locked the barn and started his long journey home; he decided to take the longer route home, using the main road. When he reached his home, he could see Doctor Allman sitting on the front porch in an armchair taken from the kitchen. James quickly approached the doctor. He told him to go directly into his father's room, there was a dim candle wall light on, but he could see fairly well anyway. Mama came up to James and picked him up in her arms, hugged and kissed his face; he could tell she had been crying. Her beautiful big brown eyes were red and watery, and her face seemed drawn of all life. "Your father is waiting for you," she whispered in his ear as she gently put him down and gave James one last squeeze. He walked up to the bed; all the fear that had left his body when wild dogs were chasing him through the dark, wet forest had returned. James's heart was beating rapidly; it felt like it was going to jump out of his chest. My great-grandfather Salvatore made direct eye contact with James. "Come here, my son, come here. I need to speak to you," he said. James's father had a full head of dark brown hair that hung down over his ears or slicked back. He played a game with the kids; he would sit at the table and bend his head forward to have his long locks hang in front of his eyes and face. He would then ask John, Nancy, and my grandfather to check his head for bugs. The three of them would wildly run their hands through his hair, checking for unwanted bugs. Of course, they learned later he just loved having all of these little hands massaging his head.

"James," he said.

James interrupted him quickly. "Yes, Papa!!"

"Can you check my hair? I feel bugs crawling around in my hair." James put his hands through his father's hair and began searching and massaging, not quite as hard as he would have in the past. Somehow, James knew this was different.

"James," his father continued, "you made me proud today. I wish we had more time together. I wish you could remain a boy a little longer, that you could enjoy your childhood with no worries, no adult choices, but life isn't always what we think it's planned to be. I'm sorry for that. You did well tonight in getting the doctor, but there is nothing he can do for me now." His father, barely able to breathe, proceeded to prepare him for the inevitable. "Tonight you were forced out into the cold dark night for a reason; you took your first steps in preparation for becoming a man, the man of our family. You are going to face many challenges and obstacles along the road of life. I know that you are capable of facing what life has in store for you. Son, you made me proud today. James, you made me proud."

My grandfather's father passed away that night. He was thirty-three years old. He lost the battle of life to coal miner's disease (black lung). He left behind three young children under ten years of age, a wife who was twenty-five years young, in a town with no promise or future. My grandfather continued to make his family proud. As long as I can remember, he always looked after his mother, my great-grandmother Grace. She lived to be eighty-eight years of age and she had her whole family by her side when she passed away. He was a great son, husband, father, and unbelievable grandfather.

New York City Bowery, next stop.

My Great Grandfather
Salvatore Palame

Chapter 6

Monique

How can I write a book about my life experiences and not dedicate a chapter to my daughter Monique? Monique has been the most important part of my life for twenty-one years. From the day I knew I was going to be a father, I knew I would love her more than anything in the world, more than life itself. I always wanted to be a father for as long as I can remember, I think it goes back to when I was thirteen years old, my niece Alicia was born and I had an immediate parental connection to her. I enjoyed spending time with Alicia, taking her out to the park, or just babysitting for her when Celeste — that's Alicia's mom — needed a break.

Monique was born Saturday January 12, 1985 at 10 AM, I was in the delivery room taking pictures while Monique's mother was giving birth to her. When Monique was born, the doctor asked me to cut the umbilical cord. The umbilical cord is what feeds the fetus for nine months while it develops in the mother's uterus; all the blood and nutrients travel through the umbilical cord to feed life into the baby. When you cut the umbilical cord the baby begins to live on its own. The feelings and emotions I experienced seeing the baby being born and cutting the cord was like no other feeling I've ever experienced. At this point, I realized how much she was going to rely on me to protect and nurture her. My baby's life has just begun as well as mine, and this baby is going to be the most important part of my life. I will always be her father through good times and bad. I realized I had to change my lifestyle, I needed to be a better person. I would be required to set a good example, eventually leave a legacy that she would be proud of.

The first person I called when Monique was born was my grandfather Jim. Grandpa was in mourning for my grandma Filomena. Grandma had passed away suddenly of a heart attack two weeks earlier. The whole family was very upset about my grandma; she was the rock of the family. Grandma Filomena kept the family strong and together. Everyone respected each other because she treated all of us the same. Grandma never spoke harshly of her children or grandchildren; she loved her brothers and sister, and always spoke in the highest regard for them. Grandpa started crying when I told him I had a baby girl. We didn't name Monique right away; we couldn't agree on a name. After two days, we finally named our little baby girl Monique Phyllis Prestipino. Phyllis was in remembrance of my grandma Filomena. Monique was a wonderful baby; she was smart, happy, independent, and she slept all night. Monique loved spending time with me, and I with her. Monique was two years old and I would take her on my business trips to Florida. She was easy to travel with and it gave her grandparents a chance to spend some time with her. Her grandparents lived in Ft. Lauderdale and most of my business was in Miami, so the arrangement worked out well.

I played softball in a very competitive league in the summers. Most Sundays I couldn't leave the house for my games unless I took Monique with me. It wasn't such a big deal because my dad came to all the games and she would sit with him and watch the games. One day we were playing this team that we never got along with, and there were definitely hard feelings between a few of the guys on both teams. We had a bench-clearing brawl, and my brother Richie somehow ended up in the middle of it. Everyone was at the pitcher's mound pushing, shoving, and wrestling with each other. In the middle of the bench-clearing brawl I could see my dad trying to get a hold of someone. His two sons were involved and that's all he needed to see, so there was no stopping him. Now that I see my dad on the field, I immediately look towards the first base dugout to check on Monique. There she was, sitting on the bench, looking out onto the field, her feet dangling over the bench, like nothing was happening. "Dad," I said, "Monique, she's in the dugout by herself, get back there now." We had a good laugh about that one; it could've been on one of those funniest home videos. It actually broke up the fighting on the field.

Monique went to more Giants tailgate parties as a young kid than most people will in a lifetime. She never complained it was too cold, or it was raining, or our seats were too high in the stadium. She did complain if she thought I was drinking too many beers. Monique played hockey on a girls' traveling team, The Bridgewater Wings. The players were primarily college girls who were playing organized hockey for their schools or recently graduated and wanted to continue to play at a competitive level. Monique and I boarded a plan bound for Toronto; the Wings were heading to Toronto for a tournament. The tournament was a premium class A tournament, and the caliber of the players' skills was exceptional. As soon as we sat in our seats, Monique fell asleep; she was curled up and within minutes, out cold. When we were boarding, a woman behind me rudely pushed her young daughter and herself in front of me to get to her seat, which was directly behind mine. I gave her a look and her to me, then I just turned around and ignored her. The plane was taxiing on the runway and the flight attendant walked up the aisle telling everyone to fasten the seat belts in preparation for takeoff. The flight attendant stopped on his way back down the aisle, and I heard him say, "Please fasten your seat belt, the plane cannot take off until all passengers are buckled in." The woman got indignant and began yelling at the flight attendant. The flight attendant was taken aback, but held strong about the seat belts. I was thinking to myself, what's the big deal, just fasten the seat belt; it's for your own good anyway. The woman got up from her seat and starting ranting on, that I'm going to speak to the pilot.

"Miss, we are going to have to take this plane back to the gate if you don't sit down and buckle up." Sure enough, the flight attendant informed the captain and the plane was pushed back to the gate and security guards were called into address the incident. The woman refused to leave the plane and began screaming at the security guards. For some reason, the security guards are not authorized to physically handle or touch the passengers. The Newark Police were now called into handle the situation. Two of Newark's finest boarded the plane. They handcuffed the woman and removed her from the plane. A female flight attendant took the hand of the woman's little girl and walked her off the plane behind her mother. The woman was cursing and yelling in French at the flight attendant, passengers, and the security guards. Two hours later, the plane was ready to take off again and Monique wakes up and says to me, "Did we land yet?" I started laughing and went on to explain to her that there was a huge fight on the plane and someone was removed in handcuffs. She didn't believe me and it took the whole team to convince her that this event really happened. The tournament was a success. The girls played magnificently, and the experience was fantastic. We also had some down time to do some sightseeing, and we visited the Hockey Hall of Fame, which was the highlight of my trip. The NHL has so much history dating back to the Montréal Canadians, Toronto Maple Leafs and the New York Rangers. And players such as Bobby Hull, Bobby Orr, Rocket Richard, and many more.

Monique didn't need too many friends; she was always satisfied to play in her room with her dolls, watch TV, or read. Monique was a good student when she was young, every year up into college, her grades kept improving. While attending Red Bank Catholic High School, Monique received straight A's four years in a row. Now at Fordham, Monique is still pulling down A's. Monique works very hard and puts a lot of effort into her studies.

My daughter Monique has made my life complete, she has brought me so much joy, laughter, and a sense of reality. Being a father has taught me how to be caring, patient, and ethical. Monique and I have gone through a lot lately. Since my divorce from her mother, we have had our ups and downs; our relationship has been strained. I could've handled certain situations differently. I assumed my love for my daughter would withstand any hurt I may've caused her by moving out of our house, and to a degree, out of her life. Monique's relationship was not great with her mom, and I left her life and left her alone with her mom. Time does heal, and today Monique has a much better relationship with her mother, and we're working on ours.

Monique and me, well, it's not the same as it was, and at times, we both struggle with each other. I still think of her everyday and wonder how she's doing. Is she happy, is she going to be ok? I know her life is going to have many ups and downs, but at the end of the day, she has the potential to be whatever she wants to be. I know she could achieve success in anything she chooses, I use the word *choose* because some people aren't smart enough, don't have work ethic, or are just not capable of doing what they choose. Monique will be able to plant her own business model and future, I'm sure of it.

No matter what's happens between Monique and me, we have many moments that no one can ever take away from us: our love for each other, the hundreds of weekends together, sporting events, Saturday afternoon movies, surprise visits to Grandma and Grandpa's house in Brooklyn, parades, trying to derail the New Jersey Transit train off the tracks, driving a bunch of eighth graders around in my 1964 Cadillac convertible, and most of all being each other's best friend.

Friends for life

Monique in central park

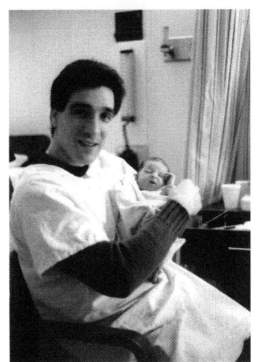

Me and Monique
two minutes old

Monique and I in Capri

Chapter 7

Under the lights

Last I remember, I was sitting in my biology classroom, preparing to take a final examination. Biology was never one of my better subjects; I failed biology twice and had to take it all over again. I need to pass this test; I do not want to take biology a third time. I'm feeling nervous, because I really don't understand any of it. I've studied for a week straight, and biology seems like advanced Greek to me.

Another concern I have is that if I fail biology, I will be in jeopardy of not making the baseball team. In order to play on the high school team, you have to pass all your subjects. I know my coach wants me to pass the test; he excused me from practice all week so I could study in place of batting practice. FDR's baseball team was not a great team. The high school had 6,000 students; it's a miracle your teachers even knew your name. The school was situated in the heart of Brooklyn, right next to the Washington Cemetery, and sandwiched between typical city neighborhoods. Our school didn't have a baseball field of our own to practice on. Actually, we used a neighboring high school's baseball field called Aramus Field to play our home games. The field had tall, high fences, a warning track, and was a major league-size field. Whenever I played in Aramus, I always altered my swing, trying to pull one out down the right field line which was 310 feet. I hit the fence a dozen times, but only managed to pop one over it once. My dad would say "Your swing is not tailored to hit them over the fence; you only know how to hit line drives." I guess that was a compliment, but it never stopped me from trying.

The night air was cool, and a soft breeze was blowing towards the outfield. The field looked slightly different; there were some stands on the first and third base line, enough to hold a few thousand people. I noticed lights were sitting atop these huge wooden poles. The lights were so bright that the field looked as though it was the middle of the day. I have seen major league ballparks in the evening, but never have I witnessed anything as bright as this field. I also noticed I am a lot younger; this was a little weird for me. I have time traveled many times before, but usually to a familiar place or a story told to me by my dad or grandfather. The more I looked around, the more familiar the field looked to me.

I was dressed in worn dungarees, shoes and a button-down white shirt. I had no idea what year I was in or why I was here standing on makeshift bleachers behind the right field fence. Before I could get comfortable and try and figure out what was going on, I heard some other kids about my age coming towards me. I would guess I was about twelve years old at this moment.

"Hey, what you doing up there? You're sitting in our seats." I looked over to where the voices were coming from and saw there were three young black kids about the same age as me approaching me quickly.

I didn't quite know what to say, so I said "I'm getting ready to watch the baseball game."

One of the boys shouts back at me "Do you know who is playing here tonight? What are you doing here anyway?"

"I'm here to watch a baseball game," I replied. I wasn't sure why I was here, but at the moment, it sounded good, and I figured I'd go with it; at least that was what I thought. The three boys were upon me and looked very suspiciously at me.

One of the boys says, "This is a baseball game for the Negro League. Monarch Grays are playing the Black Yankees."

According to my recollection, the year was 1935 and the Negro League had some of the best baseball players in the world playing in it. I was about to watch a baseball game between two of the greatest Negro League teams ever, the Monarch Grays and Black Yankees. That is, if I can convince my new friends not to beat me up or tell me to leave.

"So what you doing here I asked you?"

"I want to watch a game," I answered.

"Do you know white people don't come to watch these games?"

"No, I didn't know that. Why would they not want to watch Satchel Paige pitch and Josh Gibson hit?"

"How do you know Josh Gibson and Satchel Paige?"

"I've read about them in many books." I just realized at this moment there are no books written about these players, at least not in 1935.

"What books you talking about?"

"The newspaper," I replied. "I know that Satchel Paige is the greatest pitcher ever and eventually someday, he will pitch in the major leagues. I know Josh Gibson will be known as the black Babe Ruth and will be the first person to hit a baseball out of Yankee Stadium."

"How do you know this stuff, you weird or something?"

Just as I was getting ready to plead with them to let me stay, one of the other boys says, "Ok, you can share our bleacher seats and watch the game with us. Do you know Babe Ruth?"

"Not really, but I've read a lot about him also. I know he thinks Josh Gibson is a great ball player and would love to have him as a teammate on the New York Yankees."

One of the other boys shouted back to his friends, "See, I told you Babe Ruth knows about the Negro League."

The game was about to start; the players were on the field warming up. I couldn't help but notice how gracefully the players moved about the field. The way they fielded ground balls and ran and threw was such a beautiful sight to see. You can tell these men loved what they were doing; they were playing baseball for the fun of it. I'm sure all of these baseball players had full-time jobs during the day and still played baseball eight times a week during the season. Not many people know that the Negro League invented night baseball. In fact, they were the first to play baseball under the lights. When the Negro League started to take off, and draw paying fans, the Negro League team owners would rent major league stadiums such as Ebbits Field and the Polo Grounds to play their games. The stadiums could hold thousands of people; the only problem was that the major league teams played their games during the day. The stadiums were rented out at night, and large portable generators and lights were installed on the roof of the stadium just for the game and removed by morning. That is how night baseball was started, the Negro teams played under the lights in front of thousands of fans.

The starting pitcher for the Grays was Satchel Paige, the most popular black baseball player until Jackie Robinson broke the baseball color barrier. Satchel had what it took: skill, class, confidence, and a coolness unmatched by anyone. Satchel was great to watch; you never knew what he would do next. I could see the three boys I was sitting in the right field bleachers with were memorized by him. The game was a close game; the Grays were winning two runs to one and the game was moving along quickly. Satchel was going through the lineup as if he was pitching from forty-five feet instead of sixty. The Black Yankees were having trouble hitting the ball in play, let alone pulling it. The only player on the Yankees to connect on Satchel was Josh Gibson. Gibson always felt he would be the first black player to break the color barrier, but he never did. Poor health and age sneaked up on him before he had a chance to prove he was a great one.

Josh, in his second at-bat against Satchel, blasted a solo home run over the left field fence, a good 450 feet away from home plate. Satchel did not enjoy that moment and was barking something to Josh as he ran around the bases. Josh Gibson never even looked over at Satchel. The game few by; it was a great pitching duel. The top of the ninth inning, the Yankees had the eighth, ninth, and leadoff hitters due up this inning. Satchel quickly retired the eighth and ninth batters, when the most unusual and outrageous event was about to happen. Satchel called his fielders in for a quick meeting at the mound. There seemed to be some confusion and disagreement going on. After the short meeting with the pitcher, the players all turned around and ran back to their positions. Satchel stepped on the mound and gestured to his fielder to sit down. The whole infield sat down on their gloves, while Satchel was preparing to intentionally walk the next three batters to load the bases, with the greatest Negro League hitter of all time coming to the plate. Josh Gibson was the only hitter this night to hit Satchel hard. Satchel could've ended the game, striking out the leadoff hitter if he wanted to. No, instead Satchel chose to load the bases and face the black Babe Ruth. As Josh walked to the plate, he looked confused, shocked; he had to be thinking Satchel has surely lost his mind now.

As Josh stepped to the plate, Satchel yelled to him, fast ball down the middle of the plate. Josh was too smart for Satchel; he knew that wasn't his best pitch. Satchel winds and delivers a fastball down the middle of the plate. Josh takes it for strike one. Satchel glares down towards Josh one more time and yells "Fast ball down the middle of the plate." Josh has no reaction as he sets himself in the batter's box and is set to hit. Strike two right down the middle of the plate. Josh takes another fastball. Josh Gibson is the best hitter in baseball; most pitchers are afraid to throw a fastball at Josh. Most of the time, he gets curve balls away and out of the strike zone. Josh is set again in the batter's box. This time you can see a look of anger and determination on his face. Satchel, standing on the mound, looks around the field at his infield sitting on their gloves, and now gestures to the outfielders to come in and sit in the dugout. The outfielders trot off the field and into the dugout. Josh Gibson now has steam coming out of his ears. Satchel bears down at Josh and yells "Fastball down the middle of the plate." Satchel winds and delivers a fastball down the middle of the plate, the most beautiful pitch a hitter could hit.

"Strike three!" shouts the umpire. Josh Gibson strikes out with the bases loaded, two outs, the infielders sitting on their gloves, the outfielders sitting in the dugout, and not once did Josh Gibson ever swing the bat. Josh Gibson took three straight down-the-middle fastballs from Satchel Paige and never did his bat leave his shoulder. Josh Gibson angrily turned and walked away from the plate and back to the dugout. Game over, Monarch Grays 2, Black Yankees 1.

Satchel Paige, the master pitcher, the master mind player, strikes out JOSH GIBSON on three straight pitches. Now this is baseball at it best; this is how legends are created and history written.

My new friends were jumping and howling at the event that just happened in real life in front of us all. I've read about this event in books and articles about Satchel, but I could never appreciate the excitement and tension of this moment until now. I began to celebrate along with my new friends. I didn't want the moment to stop, but I knew as soon as I thought that, I would be back in my time.

Sitting back at my desk. "Put your pencils down, please make sure your name is on the test, and pass the final examinations to the front of the room." All I can hear is the teacher saying "the test is over" and "please pass your test to the front." I don't remember writing my name on the test, let alone taking it. I thought for sure I am taking biology again next year.

I got a 95 on my biology exam, and if you ask me if I remember one question from that test, I will absolutely tell you no.

Satchel Paige was the greatest pitcher of all time in the Negro League

Satchel pitching for the Cleveland Indians

The Famous Josh Gibson

The greatest Hitter ever in the Negro leagues

Josh Gibson hit over 800 Homeruns in his career

Chapter 8

Upstate New York

I was relaxing very comfortably on my couch this very cold winter Saturday in February 1996. I have been traveling quite a bit for my company lately, and to be home doing absolutely nothing felt great. I was watching some old black-and-white movie on TV about a guy whose whole life is caving in around him. The lead character is contemplating throwing himself off of the bridge, I think it's a wonderful world or something, I think James Stewart is the actor.

The air seemed so fresh and clear; I can't remember ever breathing air this fresh and clean that I actually noticed how clean it felt. I know when I've visited New York City in the 1920s, the air didn't feel that clean, even back then. Something's different about the air I was breathing now. I didn't recognize my surroundings, but as usual, I wasn't surprised to see myself standing on a baseball field among a bunch of strange people. I was wearing a pair of slacks with suspenders and a white tank top shirt. I had on a pair of brown square-tip shoes with an unusual amount of shoelace. I was standing in the second base position between first and second, and of course I had a glove in my hand, one that felt like a kid's glove. It barely fit my hand; I couldn't imagine trying to catch a baseball with it. I looked around and everyone on the field and on the benches along the foul lines was dressed similarly. There were girls in the small bleachers on the first base side of the field. They were all dressed in very hip Capri type pants, with blouses, and spiked heel shoes. The person up at the plate just hit a wicked ground ball to the left of the shortstop. I glanced over and noticed there was runner on first and he was headed towards second base. My natural reflexes took over. I had to cover second base, and if there weren't two outs, I would have to try and turn over a double play. I quickly shuffled over to second base in anticipation of the shortstop going way over to his right in the hole between third and short, catching the ball, and throwing it to me at second. Not to my surprise, the shortstop glided to his right so fast and gracefully, backhanded the hard-hit ground ball, came up and threw a perfect strike to me at second base. The ball landed right in the middle of my small mitt, I stepped on second base, took a back step and threw a perfect strike to first base for a beautiful 5-4-3 double play. That is box score talk for a double play from the shortstop to the second baseman to the first baseman. The hand that was in the mitt stunk badly; the glove had very little padding protection and the ball seemed to just hit square on my palm. The inning over, we all trotted off the field. A few of the guys came by and patted me on the back, "nice back step there," "I never quite seen that move before." I said thanks and continued off the field. The rest of the guys were yelling over to the shortstop, "great play, Nat," "nice pickup, Nat," "that a way, Nat." I should've known that the shortstop was Nat; Nat Prestipino, my dad. I recognized his style, grace, and the way he moved towards the ball immediately; I've seen him demonstrate the 5-4-3 double play a hundred times before. I've seen my dad play baseball before, but whenever I see him playing in his youth, I am in total awe. In fact, when watching my dad as a young man playing shortstop I can see a strong resemblance to my brother Richie in him. My brother has that same speed and graceful gliding or shuttle movement to their left and right that my dad had. I didn't quite have the gracefulness of my dad and my brother, but I will say this much: I did have a stronger arm than both of them. That is why I eventually moved to the outfield later on in my playing days. My dad looked so good, I could tell he was having a good time today; he was smiling and talking to the girls on the sidelines, enjoying a summer afternoon on the ball field. I know where we are now; we're in upstate New York in the Catskills Mountains. It has to be summer and I'm not quite sure of the year yet. My dad and his friends spent many summer weekends in the Catskills. I heard all the stories and good times they had. My dad came over to me during the inning and complimented me on turning over the double play. "My name is Natale, everyone calls me Nat, nice to meet you.

I said, "My name is Gary and it's nice to meet you too."

My dad asked, "Is this your first time up here?"

I replied, "Yes, and I really love the air up here." We both laughed at the same time, and said "It beats the city smog." We finished the game and everyone gathered their belongings and headed back to the bungalows.

"Hey Gary, where you been all day?" I looked over to see this young man in his mid-twenties walking over to me. "We have to get ready for dinner soon."

I said "Yes, I'm starving; I worked up an appetite playing baseball."

"You were playing baseball? You don't know how to play baseball, you're a musician and you play the Base. And if you don't get cleaned up and ready within the next hour, you're going to have to play your sets all night with an empty stomach." You really are new to this circuit. Where did you say you performed before?

I responded back to my band mate, "Are you sure?" And at this point, I really didn't care how stupid I was going to sound, so I asked him what his name was.

"Bernie, Bernie Kats, you idiot. What, did you get hit in the head with a baseball?"

"Never mind, Bernie. Take me back to our living quarters, please. I don't think I feel that great."

"You better be able to play tonight, or else you don't get paid and they're never going to ask you back again."

Once in my room, I threw myself on the bed and mumbled "What am I going to do now?" I fell asleep for a few minutes and was woken up by another band member walking into the room. I got up from the bed, showered, and cleaned up. I had a perfectly pressed tuxedo hanging on the back of my door; I figured it was mine and slipped into it. Luckily, it fit perfectly; actually, I like the way it looked. I was young, in good shape, tan, and felt good being in a tuxedo. The only problem I had a head of me was I had to play the base. I always wanted to be in a band when I was a teenager, but I never had any real musical talent, except for mandatory music classes in High School which I played the Base for two years. Well, I missed dinner tonight; the country clubs really don't cater to the help. I showed up at the dining room a few minutes after 5 PM and the tables were already being reset for the paying customers. That meant no dinner for me tonight. I didn't exactly have much of an appetite anymore; in fact, my stomach was kind of upset.

The guests started filing into the dining room about 5:45 PM. I recognized a few people from the baseball game earlier in the day walking into the dining room. I was not scheduled to play for the dinner crowd. The band's piano player was playing some classic tunes as a backdrop for the diners. I was enjoying the music very much, when I started to realize I was going to have to either remember how to play the Base in about two hours, leave, or see a miracle. It's 8 PM and now I'm wishing for a miracle, because I know I'm not leaving anytime soon. I feel so strong and alert, I actually have music in my head. I can't explain it, but I'm hearing tunes and I seem to have a beat going on. This is very weird; I'm putting my faith in a miracle.

I'm standing in the back row of the stage along with the other members of the band; everyone is tuning up their instruments and getting ready for the night of music and dance to begin. The ballroom is beautiful, chandeliers are hanging from the ceiling, mirrors are on the walls, and tables are scattered around the dance floor. The dance floor is huge; I've never seen a dance floor quite so big in my life. I guess they're expecting a large crowd. It's time; the lights are dim, people are at the bar socializing, drinking, and smoking; lots of smoke in the air.

The band leader gets up and faces the band, "and a one and a two," waving his hand. The band begins to play. This seems all so familiar to me. I immediately pick up the tune and begin to play the Base. I am playing a tune I never heard before, but it sounds great. The band is a ten-piece musical group that, from what I can see, has been together for quite some time. The music sounds awesome. For now, we are just playing some soft background music. Soon enough, we change the tempo and we're playing more upbeat tunes that sound like swing. The dance floor fills instantly and just about everyone has grabbed a partner and is dancing. The scene is magnificent; all these young, very attractive people dancing and swinging their partner around the dance floor. The best thing about all of this is I'm playing the Base and I'm having the time of my life. I was born to be a musician; well, that is at least how I feel now.

The band takes a break; I'm feeling pretty good about myself. I have this newfound talent and I can't help but notice a lot of the girls in the dance hall are smiling and flirting innocently with me. I feel like Bon Jovi or Elvis. Ok, I'm getting a little ahead of myself. Actually, I do have a motive; I'm looking for my dad. I want to say hello to him again, show off to him that I can play second base and the Base. I spotted my dad standing over at the smaller bar towards the end of the room. He is talking to three young girls; their backs are all facing me. My dad is facing me and makes eye contact with me. Immediately he smiles, waves his arms up, and gestures for me to come over to his group. I walk directly over to him. He shouts over, "Good evening, Gary. You didn't tell me you were in the band. Let me introduce you to some friends of mine." As I approached my dad and the three girls, they all turned around to greet me. To my surprise, my eyes can't believe it, I know these three young ladies, and they are Norma, Marie, and Grayce, as in my aunt Norma, Aunt Marie, and my mother, Grayce Palame. They look unbelievable. I quickly look at Aunt Norma and Aunt Marie, but can't help but notice my mother. She is beautiful, tall, dark, and lean. She has thick, long, curly, jet-black hair, red lipstick; she is very dark, just like my brother Richie. All three ladies are so young; I don't remember them looking like this. My mom looks a little like my niece Alicia; it's amazing the resemblance. She also has the same eyes as my niece Kristina.

"Hello, Gary, nice to meet you. So you're in the band," my Aunt Norma asked?.

I stuttered a bit and finally said yes. I couldn't stop looking at my mom. I've gotten used to seeing my dad in the past, and whenever I run into him, I can usually find something to say, but this is the first time I've met my mother. I can see that my dad is interested in my mother and she in him, even though they are keeping their distance. I hung around and talked to my aunts and mother for a few minutes, and then excused myself to go back to my band. I was shocked, I've heard the story so many times from my parents about the time they met upstate, and how my dad knew my aunt Norma and my aunt Marie from when he lived in Florida. Evidently, he met them in Florida when he was living there with his friend, Louie Slalzo. When my dad met up with my aunts and my mother at the upstate resort, he assumed he knew my mom and kissed her hello. She didn't take that kindly to his forward behavior and made a point to tell him so. My dad, an easygoing person, didn't take offense; he kind of laughed and enjoyed my mom's attitude.

I was wondering when I was going to leave. I was not feeling weak or disoriented; again I was feeling pretty darn good. So I got back on the stage and prepared for my second set of the night. Who knew what was ahead? I was witnessing a miracle, as far as I was concerned. To tell you the truth, I was having a great time, I enjoyed the music, the people, and the atmosphere. I was figuring the year had to be around 1948 to 1950, I'm not quite sure. My brother Richie was born in 1953 and I can't remember how long my parents dated and how long they were married before Richie was born.

The second set began and the dance floor was again packed with young people dancing, only at this time of night, the dancing was slow dancing and the couples were out on the dance floor dancing closely to each other. All of a sudden, I was able to see a special couple walk on to the dance floor, my mom and dad. My dad took my mother's hand and put his other hand on her back and literally carried her around the dance floor as if her feet were not touching the floor. Not only was my dad graceful on the baseball field, but he could dance with great finesse, class, and charm. They had to be the most handsome couple on the dance floor that night. I was watching the beginning of a family, a love and life partnership forming right before my eyes. What a night for Grayce Palame, who met her Prince Charming, and Natale Prestipino, who met his beautiful, smart, very young, independent future bride and life partner. I know it was a night

I will never forget, seeing my mother and father so young, innocent, not knowing what lay ahead for both of them.

My movie had ended and the volume was very high on the TV. A commercial was playing for a sky resort in the Poconos. I got up off the couch and walked over to get my portable phone. I dialed up my mom and dad's phone number. The phone rang four times and the answering machine came on. The message said "You have reached the home of Nat and Grayce Prestipino. We are not home, we are unavailable to answer the phone. Please leave your name, phone number, and time you call, God Bless."

God bless my parents; I think every child should be able to go back in time and see their parents before they have responsibilities, family, illness, and old age. Seeing my mom so young and carefree was a great experience; she was truly a beautiful young lady, and my dad was a very lucky man to have met and married her.

Mom and Dad at a friends Wedding

Chapter 9

The worst day of my life

The worst day of my life was preceded by the most heart-wrenching, hectic summer ever in my life. The summer started out with Janet and me buying a house in Rumson, New Jersey. The house was a charming, beautiful, turn-of-the-century Victorian. We instantly fell in love with the house, and no matter how many other houses we looked at, we came back to this one. The only problem was that we still had to sell our condo, which we were assured we would have no problem selling. I'll leave it at that for now. Actually holding on to the condo for the summer would've worked out great for us. It gave Janet and me time to do some renovations to our new home. We had all the carpets pulled up and the floors sanded and stained. We had all the wallpaper removed and every room, wall, and ceiling in the house painted. The condo had a great pool, so staying in the condo for the summer would allow us to utilize the pool.

My dad's health was gradually declining over the last couple of months. My father had had two major heart surgeries over the last twenty years. Both surgeries were considered a great success and a life-saving procedure. He enjoyed full recovery after each one and was able to go back to his normal life and activity. Of course, he always had to monitor his blood levels and keep to a healthy diet, along with some light exercise. My mom made sure he ate healthy, stayed active, kept a good attitude, and took his medicine religiously. He visited his heart doctor every three months for routine physicals. We finally convinced him to stop driving because his eyesight was getting worse. People would blow their horns or drive up beside him and flip him the finger because he was driving so slowly. This would infuriate my dad, and my mom would have to endure some road rage from him.

The only problem my dad had that was not under his control was asbestos poisoning of his lungs. He had worked in the Brooklyn Navy Yard many years ago and was exposed to asbestos . There were many class action suits filed to his surprise that he was involved in, , he never knew this was killing people and so many of them were suing the companies that caused it. The spring of 2004, he started having trouble breathing, he couldn't catch his breath, and it was starting to wear on him. His breathing problems escalated when he was lying down or sleeping. This is where his problems got worse. My dad was always a great sleeper, and when his sleep was being interrupted with bouts of gasping for air, this was not good for him. Of course my mom arranged for him to see a lung specialist immediately. My dad was checked thoroughly by Doctor Salar, who just happened to be the best lung doctor in all of Brooklyn. So my dad was in good hands, we hoped and prayed. The asbestos was getting worse and he had to go on oxygen almost 24/7. This kept my dad in the house more than he was used to. July and August were the best months of the year for my dad; he loved to watch the New York Yankees every day on TV. He also followed and supported a local softball team. They were group of guys in their thirties who played in a very competitive softball league with a winner-take-all cash championship prize. Sometimes, one of the ball players would pick him up before the games at home, or drop him back home after the game. He enjoyed these softball games, and the guys loved having him around; they were all like his sons.

July and August were terrible months for my dad, my mom, and the family. My dad was not eating, no matter what my mom made for him, he didn't want to eat. That was not a good sign. We all tried talking to him, and he always assured us he was trying his best. The visits to the hospital began to be more frequently. His legs would swell up with water; there's a medical term for that. His legs were so swollen, you couldn't put a slipper or a sock on his foot. I spoke privately to Doctor Salar about my father's conditions, and he told me his prognosis did not look good. When my mom found out I spoke to Doctor Salar, she pushed me to tell her everything he said. Of course I lied and told her the doctor felt he could help Daddy and he would improve. I couldn't face telling her the truth; it would've devastated her. The doctors in the hospital put him on Lasix medication and heavy antibiotics, and the swelling would gradually go down. Once the swelling went down, he would be released and sent home. A week later, or sometimes even sooner, he would get an attack and my mom would rush him back to the emergency room. Sometimes they would keep him overnight, or release him that same night. Janet and I most times would jump in the car and head to Brooklyn. My mom was by herself and we wanted to be there to support her. My niece Alicia was always there for my dad as well; she had two young children and always seemed to find a way to get to the hospital. I remember one night we had the whole family in the emergency room, Alicia, my daughter Monique, Mom, Janet, and me, and of course my dad. He was very upset because that weekend was Father's Day and we had all planned to go to dinner with him. When his personal doctor walked into the emergency room, to our surprise at two o'clock in the morning, he looked at all of us and said "How did you all get in here?" Then he stopped and said "I don't want to know." He was actually in a good mood for being in the hospital on Friday night at 2 AM. He examined my father and said "I'll wait for some tests to come back, but I think you'll be able to go home today." The smile on my father's face said it all; he was relieved and happy, as were we all. The doctor and my mom have this love-hate relationship. She loves telling him what he should be doing and he hates hearing her telling him what to do. The doctor loved to tell us that he prescribes Valium to his patience that come to see him, but when Grayce, (that's my mom) comes to visit him, he takes a Valium. We all laugh, including my dad and my mom. Mom is pretty good at taking a joke, especially since we all knew my dad was going home and the doctor was in no hurry to get home himself, and was enjoying our bedside chat.

In between hospital stays, my dad and mom managed to come to New Jersey to celebrate my aunt Vinnie and uncle Andy's eightieth birthdays. They had a nice afternoon dinner at a restaurant close to their development. My dad did not look good, and he was feeling so weak, I had to hold him when we walked in. But he still had that signature smile of his on his face and put up a good front. His kid sister Marie was there, so I know he tried his best to look like he was enjoying himself and that nothing was wrong. Marie was the kid sister, some fourteen years younger than my dad. I guess she was the baby of his family, and he always treated her special. That's not to say he didn't love his sister Vinnie; they were very close too. I have to say I never saw them argue once. In fact, both of my dad's sisters put him on pedestal and treated him with great respect.

That night, my parents were going to sleep at Janet's and my place. We had a comfortable two-bedroom condo that my mom and dad loved to visit. In fact, Janet, Mom, and I were talking about the first time they slept over. The building blew an electrical generator, and the fire department came and ordered the building to be evacuated. My mom came over to me and started shaking me to wake up; we have to leave. It was six in the morning and of course she was wide awake and had been in the halls talking to the residents of my building. She told me, "Go wake up your father and help get him get dressed and I'll be outside checking on what's going on."

She dashed out of the apartment and took off down the hall. I went into the bedroom to wake my father, who was in a deep sleep, and to boot, his hearing aids were not in his ears.

I start to softly shake my dad. "Dad, wake up, Dad, wake up."

He opens his eyes and says, "What are you doing? Why are you waking me up? And where is your mom?"

"Dad, there is a fire in the building and we have to leave. You need to get up now, and Mom is outside directing the fire trucks in the parking lot." That poor man just sat on the edge of the bed and stared straight ahead for a few minutes. Eventually, we all had a good laugh about that day.

On our way home from the birthday party, I asked my dad if he felt well enough to see the new house. I told him the house is a mess with painter's drop cloths and equipment all over the place. He of course said yes; let's go see the new house. He could barely walk and did not have the oxygen connected to him, but he pulled himself out of the car and walked up the first flight of stairs to the first floor. He walked throughout the first floor with me holding him up. "It's going to be a beautiful house, son; I know you're going to make it look great." Then he says, "Let's go upstairs." Note that the stairs had paper, plus drop cloths on them protecting them from paint and chemicals that were being used to remove the wallpaper, and were fifteen steps steep. He could barely go one step at a time, but he forced himself up the stairs. I was starting to fill up with emotion; I was trying to hold back my tears and was getting very upset. I could read his mind; he knew he wasn't going to see this house ever again and he wanted to make sure he walked through the entire house. Seeing my dad like this was painful; he was always so strong and positive about life. We got back to the car and he was exhausted and out of breath. Janet was having trouble holding back her tears and I could see she was crying. My dad still managed to tell Janet and me that he loved the house and he was proud of us. We went back to the condo and we settled in and actually had a nice evening talking and watching TV. We hooked up the oxygen, and that helped my dad breathe a lot easier that night.

This routine went on all summer and it was starting to take its toll on both my mom and dad.

By the end of August, the lung doctor had spoken to me again in private and indicated that my dad was a very sick man and he had no way of knowing how long he had to live. It could be months or weeks. He promised he would keep him comfortable and keep the communication open with me. I never told my mom about my second conversation with the doctor; I did tell Janet and Alicia. I didn't say too much to my brother

Richie either, because he was in Florida and I couldn't give him specific details anyway.

It was the week before Labor Day weekend, and it was a bad week for my dad. We all spent a couple of long nights at the hospital. My mom was there around eighteen hours a day, it seemed. She was not looking healthy herself. It was Friday and I told my mom I wasn't going to come to the hospital today; I really needed to go home and take care of some chores. My friend Michelangelo called me early Friday morning; he said, "Come on, let's go see your dad in the hospital. I haven't seen him and love to visit." I explained that I was exhausted and wasn't going today. Michelangelo persisted and I said "Yes, let's go during lunch." We took the train ride to Brooklyn and walked the four or five blocks over to the hospital. I warned Michelangelo that my dad was not the same as he remembered. Michael and I walked into the room, to our surprise, my dad was sitting up in bed, the oxygen was not connected, and he was reading the *Post*. My aunt Marie and uncle Frank were in the room talking to him also. He looked great; he was alert, talking, and joking. His smile was back on his face.

"Hello number two son and three son Michelangelo Graziano!" he shouted out as we walked in.

Michael and I spent about forty-five minutes with my dad and we had a great conversation. When it was time to leave, I said "Dad, I got to go back to work. I'll call you later," and hugged and kissed him good-bye. Michael went over and kissed my dad and hugged him as well. My dad just smiled and said to me before I left, "Remember, straighten them all out, keep them in line."

I traveled quite a bit for my work over the years and no matter where I was, whether I was out of the country or in another state, when I called my parents to say hello, my dad would get the phone and say, "So you straighten everybody out." I remember one day calling him from Frankfurt where I was meeting a big client, and this particular customer was just killing us. Later on, talking to my dad, he said "I know you took care of everything." He had such confidence in me, even though he didn't really know what I did, but he knew I was the best at it.

Since my dad was doing so well Friday, I decided to go to Michelangelo's house on Saturday evening with Janet. Jim Roberts was going to be there also, and I haven't seen him and his wife in a while. Our plans were changed on Saturday morning. Alicia called and said Grandpa was not doing well. Janet and I immediately drove back to Brooklyn. We spent the night at the hospital.

I called my brother when I got home that night and told him it was time to plan a trip to New York. I wasn't sure how long he had, but his condition was serious.

Sunday night, my niece called me again and told me she was at the hospital and that I should get here quick. I could tell she was nervous and needed me to be with her. It was a terrible night, my dad was in agony all night, and Alicia, Janet, and I stayed up by his side all night long. At 4:30 in the morning, we all agreed I would go get my mom. I remember walking into the house just before 5 AM and seeing my mother awake, fully dressed, just sitting in the living room. She didn't know at this time I had spent the whole night at the hospital with Dad. I said "Mom, get ready, we got to go to the hospital. I've been with Dad all night and it's time to go see him." Her reaction will be with me forever. Her entire body shook with fear; I thought she might faint. She didn't, she got herself together and we left for the hospital.

Miraculously, his condition stabilized in the morning once again, and he was well enough to have bowl of cereal.

That night, I called Richie again and said he couldn't wait till Wednesday anymore, that he needed to get here first thing in the morning. Richie arrived Tuesday morning and went straight to the hospital. Janet and I went home that night.

Wednesday, September 15: Normally, we take the ferry service to the city, but Janet and I decided to drive into the city that morning so we would be able to go see my dad after work.

Around 10:30 AM, Alicia called me and told me to get to the hospital as soon as possible; my dad was calling for his mother and me. I called Janet and told her we had to leave now. She immediately packed up and met me at the parking garage. I don't think I was ever this nervous or scared in my entire life. During the summer, I had moments where I wasn't so strong and I would break down and cry. I loved and admired my dad more than anything or anybody I ever met. I was and I am so proud to carry his family name (*Prestipino*). I have so many fond memories of my father that I believe will keep him in my thoughts every day for the remainder of my life. I thank God I had Janet who stood by me the whole time. She was great, she understands family, love, and people's feelings. If you knew Janet as I do, this was so difficult for her to be strong; she is not the person who can control her emotions. She is usually the one who breaks down and cries . I don't think she ever experienced anything quite like this in her life. We arrived at the hospital and my dad had everyone around him; you could see he was very uncomfortable. Alicia, Paul, Monique, Monique's friend Nick, Richie, Mom, Janet, and me. My dad spotted me and called me over to him. He told me he loved me very much, that he was proud of me, and that I was a good son. I think he thanked me for being there for him also, I can't remember. He told me he had one more thing to ask me. "Son, you take care of your mother for me; I know I can count on you."

"I will, Dad," I said. "I love you so much and I always will."

Shortly after, my dad went into a deep sleep.

The rest of the day, the whole family stayed by his side, rubbing him, praying for him, talking to him, telling him how much we loved him. I'm not sure how much he was understanding or if he heard us. At about 8:30 Wednesday night, he starting breathing heavy and the fluid in his lungs started make sounds. We all gathered around and put our hands on him and started telling him we loved him. I was standing even with his head with my brother right next to me. I'm not sure where everybody else was standing. My mom was having a hard time looking at him and had to sit down, I think her legs were giving in., Janet went over to her and put her arms around my mom and was consoling her. That poor woman was about to lose her husband, her life partner, her battle to keep him alive; he was everything to her, he was dying. At 8:40 PM Wednesday, September 15, 2004, my father, Natale Prestipino, the best father, husband, grandfather, and person you would ever meet, stopped breathing. I will never forget that moment for the rest of my life, the look on his face, saying goodbye forever.

The worst day of my life was when I had to say goodbye to my dad, the greatest dad a boy and a man could have ever had.

Me, Richie, Dad and Mom celebrating Dads birthday.
We were all very happy. We were always happy when Richie
was in town and the whole family was together.

Chapter 10

Punch ball

Growing up in Brooklyn as a kid was amazing; there was no other experience like it in the world. For the longest time in my life, I actually felt sorry for people who didn't live in Brooklyn. How ridiculous is that! As a kid in Brooklyn, you had to be creative to keep yourself busy. My friends and I made up many games to keep us occupied during the long summers or after school in the winter. We played games such as muffreeze, asses up, hide and go seek, stickball, punch ball, and Johnny on the pony. Muffreeze was a game you played in the school yard; the schools had these big circles painted on the concrete for the dance festivals every spring. Anywhere from five to ten kids would get into the circle. One person would be it and the rest of the kids would have to remain frozen. The person who was it would walk around and try to get one of frozen kids to move. Once that person moved, he would yell his name and everyone for start punching him till he counted 1, 2, 3, etc. 10 and yell muffreeze. Now that person would be it and he would now try and get another person to move. This game went on for hours and usually ended in someone getting into a real fight.

Asses up was a game of handball you played against the school yard wall. Whoever lost would have to kneel on their knees against the wall and have the rest of the guys throw a Spalding ball at your butt. Yes, I know what you're thinking, very imaginative games to keep a city kid busy. It's a wonder we ever amounted to anything. I have to say my favorite neighborhood game was punch ball; I loved playing punch ball. Punch ball could be played in the school yard, on a city street, or in an alleyway between two apartment buildings. I always enjoyed playing punch ball between two apartment buildings. The width between the buildings was approximately twelve feet. You had a first, second, third, and home just like any other field, just that it was very narrow. The rules did vary at times. Sometimes you could just punch the ball anywhere you wanted except on the roof, sometimes you weren't allowed to punch a ball against the apartment building exterior walls. There was always a group of kids willing to play punch ball, so the competition was fierce. The board of education ran after-school programs and they had organized punch ball leagues. I played in these leagues for a short time, but for the most part, I didn't participate in them because I was never allowed in the afternoon centers. I started out as an innocent good kid, but I was doomed from the beginning. The day I joined the afternoon center, I was about seven years old, excited, and couldn't wait to attend the after-school program. I remember filling out the form and handing it to Mr. Lipkin. Mr. Lipkin was a nasty, angry man. I can't imagine why he wanted to run an after-school program, and he hated most of the kids. Mr. Lipkin accepted my information form, looked at the name on the form, and asked me: "Are you related to Richard Prestipino?"

I looked up at him and said "Yes, that is my older brother," with a big smile on my face. "Do you know him?"

"Oh yes, I know him, and I'm going to tell you right now, you're on probation and I'm going to watch you very closely. You do one thing wrong and you're out of here for life."

I almost swallowed my tongue; I couldn't believe what this man was saying this to me. No one ever yelled at me, I always did what I was supposed to do, like I said earlier, I was a good kid. My brother, however, was always in trouble at the center. I didn't care what Mr. Lipkin thought of my brother, because I admire and look up to him. Long story short, I didn't survive at the after-school center, or for that matter the summer school program either. So my organized punch days were over early in my life. I was blamed for everything that was broken inside the center, and anything that was stolen from the center. Kids stole basketballs, punch balls, bats, crayons, etc. I never lifted anything for myself until I started getting blamed, then I stole everything I could get my hands on, and gave it all away to the neighborhood kids. I never kept any of it for myself; my dad wouldn't be very happy about it, so I never took anything home for me.

Back to my story: Let me tell you about the last day I played punch ball. My friends and I were getting ready to play a game of punch ball against the 50th Street boys; we were the 52nd Street boys. Back then we didn't have much imagination on neighborhood names or gang names like they do today. We belonged to a block or an avenue, and that's what you were known for. Our game was scheduled for after school and it was going to take place on 52nd Street between 18th and 19th Avenue. The field was between two apartment buildings and the rules were everywhere was in play. Everyone was excited about the game, the weather was great, we had a few hours of light remaining, and no after-school teachers to supervise us, so for sure you knew the game was going to get out of hand. The game was moving along well, both teams had scored a bunch of runs, and the action was great. I stepped up to the plate and was looking around for where I was going to place my punch. Would I go deep and over the heads of the outfielders? Should I punch a ball high and off the building wall? I always preferred to go deep and punch it out over the heads of my opponents; it was more challenging. Just as I was about to punch, out of the corner of my eye, I see a big object falling out of the sky. Within a second, a loud, creepy swat, bang sounded and there in the middle of our punch ball field lay a man splattered all over the alleyway. I can still hear that sound. I can still see that split second of a human body falling from the sky and landing dead square in the center of our punch ball court. This person fell from the sky in an instant, landed in between all of us. Some kids ran immediately, a couple of kids actually cried. I was still standing at home plate with the ball in my hand in total shock. Someone must've called the cops, because within minutes, the police arrived and quickly put up a rope barricade around the body. The EMS ambulance arrived a short time after the cops, but just to transport the body. Typical of a Brooklyn crime scene, hundreds of people were standing around trying to find out what just happen. I left and went home for supper. To tell you the truth, I never mentioned it to my mother that I was there and witnessed it with all my friends. Another thing you do in Brooklyn! Keep your mouth shut.

Game over

I'm not sure who this person was. I heard stories he was trying to jump from one building to another, one story he was on drugs and thought he could fly. I'm not sure how anyone could know, mainly because he wasn't alive to explain. It was the last time I ever played punch ball.

Chapter 11

My first job

I just graduated from school and got this great new job with a start-up company, Southern Pacific Communications, located in downtown Manhattan. Southern Pacific is a start-up telecommunications company owned by the South Pacific Railroad. I was just out of high school and had no interest in going on to college. That in itself is a completely different story that I will tell later on in my story. Let me go on: My uncle Sal owned a restaurant in Brooklyn, and let me explain this as elegantly as possible. People of power frequent his establishment; we'll leave it at that. One day, my uncle Sal's chiropractor comes to his restaurant looking very upset and not sure what to do. Neal the chiropractor begins to tell my uncle that his son Peter, twenty-eight years old, is in big trouble. Peter is borderline genius, but a bit of a flake, to say the least. Peter drinks heavily and loves to play the ponies. Well, Neal goes on how Peter has gotten into trouble with the local loan sharks. Evidently, Peter has borrowed money from the loan sharks and is unable to keep up with the payments. I believe at this point Peter cannot leave the house, which means he can't go to work. Peter is a director of operations at Southern Pacific Communications and manages a group of twenty technicians. Neal doesn't know how to ask or say it, but he is looking for my uncle Sal to help him. "Sal, you know all these people, they eat in your restaurant all the time. Can you talk to them, and can you fix my problem?"

My uncle Sal was a very cool man. When he was sixteen years old, he enlisted in the army and my grandfather had no other choice but to agree and sign for it. Uncle Sal was wounded in Korea and came home a war hero.

The plan: My uncle Sal thought long and hard for a few minutes, and then began to explain his plan. "Neal, you know there is no way out of this; you will have to pay every penny and more. I will speak to the person holding the note over your son's head and propose a revised payment plan. You will have to get him up to date and get Peter on a payback plan. I will arrange the meeting and set the terms for your son." My uncle Sal knew these men; he knew if he asked them for mercy, they would say no, but if he came to them with terms for payback and gave them a final amount not to exceed a certain dollar amount, they would accept it. These people will take from you as long as you let them, my uncle would say. As long as it's their idea and a business agreement has been worked out, everything would be ok.

My uncle Sal brought both parties together for a meeting in the restaurant. The meeting was scheduled for one in the morning. The restaurant would be closing and they could lock the doors and discuss business. Neal, an educated Jewish man from Boropark, is living a scene right out of a 1970s gangster movie. Neal shows up at the restaurant, he is very nervous, his professional hands trembling. My uncle opens the door and greets Neal warmly. "Hi Neal, don't worry, follow my lead and calm down. Believe me, they'd rather collect money than stand outside your son's apartment all day." Uncle Sal makes the introductions, and everyone sits down at a table in the back of the restaurant. There are six people at the restaurant. Frank G is a respected man in his trade; he's known to be fair, but also fearsome . Frank grew up during the Murder Row days. The movies we are watching now were based on his character. After about forty-five minutes, a deal is struck. Neal actually seems calm and relaxed. Frank is all smiles and now is complaining about his neck and the numbness in his hand. My uncle Sal, looking very amused by the whole situation, announces to Neal, "You may have a new patient out of this whole mess." Neal's smile immediately turned to a frown. My uncle laughed out loud.

Payback: Peter, now on a payment plan, out of the house, and back to work, comes to visit my uncle to thank him for his intervention into the underworld for him.

"Hello, Sal, I just wanted to thank you for all your help. My dad told me how much you did for me and I will never forget it."

"Peter," said my uncle, "you're welcome and you're right, you'll never forget what I did for you, because I won't do it again, even if your mother comes begging to me."

"Sal, I will do anything for you, work in the kitchen, clean the floors, paint?"

My uncle, a very smart man, shouts "STOP! You do not have to do any work in my restaurant. I have one request, though; you are a big boss where you work, you can hire people, fire people, give raises to people, etc. I want you to hire my godson Gary. Gary just graduated from high school; he's a baseball player who doesn't want to play baseball. He needs a job before my sister and brother-in-law throw him out of the house."

September 9, 1976, I started working at Southern Pacific Communications. I had no experience in the telecommunication field whatsoever. I showed up at work, a nineteen-year-old kid right off the streets of Brooklyn, no formal training, hair slicked back, dressed in black slacks, silk shirt, and patent leather shoes. I swear when I opened the door to the national operation center, the place just stopped. At least six people were on shift that day. Some guy, his name I learned later was Whitie, came over to me and asked me if I was lost. I said I was looking for Peter Levy and that I was here to start work today. At that point, everyone's mouth just dropped. I said "My name is Gary Prestipino. It's a pleasure to meet everyone."

The job paid good money for those times. I was getting paid $179 a week. Take-home after taxes was $129, minus a few non-federal vigs I had to pay to my uncle a piece and a certain neighborhood organization a piece. Don't ask me why, I wasn't the person who owed the loan sharks money, just a kid starting his life. After all was said and done I had eighty bucks in my pocket to get me through the week. In those days, we got paid once a week, and it was Tuesday, which wasn't so bad, since most of my money I spent was on Friday and Saturday. This arrangement was short-lived. I explained to my uncle how I was very grateful for the opportunity, and understood all the circumstance leading up to my employment, but it had to stop. I was getting up at five in the morning to be at work before 7 AM. The rule was, you had to relieve the midnight person at least fifteen minutes before the shift ended, so I followed that rule to the T. So the vigs stopped, and I was able to keep my whole check for myself

I spent nine wonderful years at Southern Pacific Communications, better known as Sprint today. I loved the work I was doing, all the training they were giving me on the job. I began to travel, Dallas, Chicago, San Francisco, and eventually to Europe. Who would've thought Gary Prestipino from Brooklyn could travel around the world?

I have been in telecommunications since 1976, I have been involved in many startup companies; all of them, I must say, have been very successful. My name in the industry is well-respected for my accomplishments, honesty, knowledge, and most of all, professionalism. The ironic thing about the whole story is a loan shark from Brooklyn with no vision into the future, looking for a $20 a week vig, provided me a great career path, which I will never forget, and an uncle who knew to get his nephew off the streets and into an industry that was on a skyrocketing growth spurt for the next twenty-five years.

Telecommunications and technology has been the biggest growth market over the last twenty-five years. A kid from Brooklyn, New York actually was the twenty-third employee of Sprint, which is now a company with over 33,000 employees worldwide, and made the first ever international calls to Europe.

Who says you can't make a difference? Gary F. Prestipino

2005

Chapter 12

BABE Ruth

Tomorrow, my dad, Monique, and I were going into New York City to honor and celebrate the New York Yankees' victory in the 1994 World Series. Mayor Giuliani was organizing one of the biggest celebrations ever. He was having a ticker tape parade. The Yankees had just won the World Series and the city and our mayor couldn't be more delighted. Monique and I were going to drive to Brooklyn, meet my dad, and then take the train into the city. My dad was very excited about the parade; he was feeling great about the World Series, and physically, he was fully recuperated from his latest heart surgery. Life was good and he was taking it one day at a time, as he always said. My dad had an excellent outlook on life, he was happy to still be alive and able to enjoy his family, his sports, and friends. Monique was excited because I was taking her out of school, she was going into Manhattan, which she always loved to do, and she was going to see a ticker tape parade that would not be forgotten for years to come. We showed up at my parents' house early; my mom had breakfast ready for us. We didn't stay very long at the house; we wanted to get to the city early and get in a good position along Broadway so we would have a clear view of the players. I had an idea where I wanted to stand for the parade, right in front of 61 Broadway. The buildings were closely located next to each other in this area of Broadway. I knew this would be a good place for all the ticker paper to fall down from the surrounding buildings. We walked a few blocks from my parents' home in Brooklyn to the B train, which we would take into Manhattan. I had my new APS camera with me, and I was looking forward to taking pictures of all the Yankees, Monique, and my dad. The train pulled into the station and we boarded. Once on the train, I sensed something was different. The train had big, round overhead fans, straw seats, and strapped overhead grip handles. Everyone was dressed in dark grey or black overcoats, and many men were wearing Stetson hats. I knew I jumped, but I wasn't sure where and what date. I looked around the train, trying to get a glance of a newspaper headline. Maybe I could recognize an event which would place me in the year I just traveled to. This was going to be a strange journey for me; I knew this from the beginning. Sitting right next to me on the train was my dad; he was wearing a dark grey suit and the classy grey Stetson hat. My dad wore a hat better than anyone I knew. He was sharp; even at his age, he looked great in his suit and top hat. Yes, my dad is accompanying me on this jump. He is the exact same age he is in 1994. I can't explain it, but he's here with me in 19-something, taking the train somewhere. I look over at my dad and he back at me.

"So, son, what do you think is going to happen today?" I look over at him and can't speak. Ok, he knows I'm his son, something is happening today, and we're not in 1994 anymore. My dad doesn't seem to have an issue with this at all; he knows I'm his son and everything is quite normal for him. The new APS camera hanging around my neck has been replaced by a double lens reflex camera and a pocketful of flashbulbs.

"Dad, can I see the newspaper you're reading?"

"Sure, son, take a look. There's an article in the *Chicago Sun-Times* today about the Babe. The article was about how the Cubs feel they have the Babe under control and believe he is over the hill already. Can you imagine that, thinking the Babe is washed up, finished?"

I grab the paper out of my dad's hand and look at the back page. Even in the year 1932, I still looked at the back page first, before reading the news. Yes, we were in the year 1932, riding a train heading to, of all places, Wrigley Field, Chicago. I was so excited that I didn't question for a minute the situation I was enjoying tremendously. I was going with it; no way was I going to upset this jump, even with all the questions and uncertainty. One, I'm riding the train with my dad and it's October 1, 1932; two, we're going to the 1932 World Series game between the Chicago Cubs and the New York Yankees in Wrigley Field; three, my dad is being himself. There is no hint we are out of place or that anything is strange or odd about this scenario. Not once has he said "What are we doing here? How is this possible? And how did we get to Chicago?"

We're going to the World Series, I know I keep saying this, but I'm actually going to see Babe Ruth and Lou Gehrig play baseball live and in person. I know for a fact that my dad never saw Babe Ruth play baseball in person; he probably didn't have enough money to go to a game back in his youth. Another small detail I should mention is that my father has never been to Chicago; he lived most of his years in Brooklyn. The brown line pulls into the Wrigley Field train station and the crowd empties out of the train and heads straight to the stadium entrances. This looks all too familiar to me. I've been to Wrigley Field a half dozen times in the past. The stadium looks the same, just that it's much newer and cleaner, ivy is covering the outfield walls, houses are right outside the stadium, just as they are today, but they look a lot nicer now. The stadium hasn't changed a bit. I love Wrigley Field; when you visit this stadium in the year 2005, it still projects the era of 1932, and a feeling you have gone back in time.

The stadium is buzzing with excitement; the Chicago fans feel good about their team and their chances of winning. It was the third game of the series; both teams had one win apiece. We were just in time for batting practice, how great was this! The Yankees took the field first; the players ran out onto the field to begin some field drills. Two young bat boys in Cub uniforms carry two large bushels of baseballs each and place them down on the pitching mound. All along, my dad and I were just enjoying the beautiful fall day, talking baseball like we normally did at the game, when the crowd noise amplified a few levels. The Babe walked out of the dugout with two monstrous baseball bats in his hands. He was swinging the two bats to loosen up. The bats look like they were oversized fungo bats. Fungo bats are long and skinny bats used to hit practice fly balls to the outfielders. These bats were long and thick, they must've weighed fifty ounces each. I looked over towards my dad. The look on his face said it all; he was just as in awe as I was. "Dad, that's Babe Ruth, do you know that Babe Ruth is out there on the field? Look how young he looks; he's not as fat as I pictured him, though."

"Son, you're right, the Babe, and you and I are here together seeing him in person."

The Babe headed over to home plate to start taking some batting practice. No sooner did he get to the plate than Lou Gehrig comes out of the dugout and walks over towards home plate and stands on deck. The batting practice pitcher threw a few warm-ups to the catcher and then signaled for the Babe to step in. The first pitch, the Babe swings. He smashed a ball right out of Wrigley Field and into the street. The crowd roared with astonishment. The next six practice swings produced balls landing in the right-field bleachers. I couldn't believe my eyes; the exhibition of hitting the Babe was displaying for the visiting team's fans. The last ball the Babe hit landed deep in the center-field bleachers and he decided to run that one around the bases. Lou Gehrig picked up the Babe's bat and walked up to the plate. If you thought the Babe put on a show of raw power and intimidation, Lou was even more impressive. Lou hit ball after ball into every location of the outfield bleachers. If there were no fences, his line drives would've picked up speed and height and landed miles away. Lou also hit a few balls out onto the street, I think just to make a statement. If I was a Cubs fan and witnessed this display of power, I would finish my beer and hot dog and get back on the train and head home. I have never seen anything quite like this. The only thing I can compare it to is the home run derby contests they have at the All-Star Games today. The only difference is that these were mostly washed-up baseballs, water-logged or beaten to death, not the juiced-up, brand-new, never-hit baseballs they use now.

Batting practice was awesome; Dad and I were having a great time. Dad bought a scorecard and was going to keep score of the game. I remember when I was a kid, we used to buy the scorecard and keep score. I've learned so much about baseball by keeping score of every play of the game. The best was still to come, there was electricity in the air, the crowd was into every pitch, call by the umpire and play in the field. It was the fifth inning and the Babe was coming to the plate. Charlie Root was the pitcher on the mound for the Cubs. So far, he was able to contain the Babe and silence his bat. The crowd was jeering the Babe as he approached the plate. The Babe stepped into the batter's box; it looked like the Babe and the Chicago pitcher were jawing at each other. The fans were picking up on it and they began booing the Babe. The Babe kept talking to Charlie Root and Charlie Root was jawing back at the Babe. The Babe now is gesturing with his right hand; it looks like he's pointing to center field. I know what game we're at, we're at the called shot game. The Babe is pointing to the outfield and telling Charlie Root he's hitting the next pitch for a home run. At this point, the crowd is out of control, the stadium is literally rocking. Charlie Root delivers the next pitch and Babe Ruth smacks it to dead center, deep into the bleachers for a monster home run. I turn to my dad and we begin to hug each other while we are jumping up and down in wild celebration. The fans around us are not too pleased with our display of joy.

We can't believe we just witnessed the called shot; this is one of the greatest moments in baseball history. I took a flash bulb out of my pocket, inserted it into the flash attachment, stepped into the aisle, and took a photo of my father with the first base side of the infield as a backdrop. It's a good thing I remembered how to use a double lens reflex camera. My dad bought one when my brother Richie was born, and he could never figure out how to use it. When I turned eleven, I got interested in photography and started using the camera. I still have that camera today.

A big flash and pop, and we were back on our way to 1994, with my new APS camera hanging around my neck, replacing the double lens reflect that I was carrying around in 1932..

Our train pulls into Rector Street; Dad is half-asleep, and Monique is fast asleep as usual. I nudge my dad and whisper into Monique's ear, "It's our stop, we have to get up." We exit the train and head up the stairs to the street. Monique is getting excited and is walking quickly because she' in a hurry to get to Broadway so she could get in a good position to see her favorite players. Dad and I were relaxing on the steps of 61 Broadway, drinking a cup of coffee, watching Monique from a distance, and talking baseball.

We're back in 1994 again, and my father is talking to me like he always does; nothing strange is going on as far as I can tell. We talked about the old Yankees, the 1950s, and Murder Row teams of the late twenties and early thirties. I had to say something; this was too dramatic of a day not to mention it. So I started out by saying, "Dad, did you ever see Babe Ruth play baseball?" In the past, he always said no, he never had the privilege to see the Babe play in person.

"Once, son, yes once I was able to see Babe Ruth play, and it was one of the greatest moments in baseball history, one of the greatest moments in my life. I will never forget this day as long as I live." Just as I was about to speak, he interrupted me! "I think I'm going to go over and stand with my granddaughter right now, if you don't mind. "

My dad and I had ten more great years together before he had to leave for good. We talked about a lot of baseball, but never about the called shot game of 1932. You have to know the Prestipino's to understand the logic behind this , how is it possible that a father and Son could travel to another time and place and not talk about it, not think this is strange. This is our family, limited communication, secrets, fear of the truth, we just don't talk. I left it at that, he was happy, maybe too much talk of it would take away from the moment, maybe he's time travel before and it's his personal secret.

Maybe I was afraid it really didn't happen, and if I brought it up, he wouldn't know what I was talking about. You can't disregard his comments, though, about the one time he saw the Babe play. It makes you think, did the Babe really call that home run? I say yes.

I will never forget this day. How many people have the opportunity in a lifetime to spend a day like the one I had with my father and daughter?

Another wonderful day in my life.

*The babe hitting the
famous called shot*

Wrigley field

Dad and Me at the Yankee parade, Monique is behind the camera

Chapter 13

A trip to the city

I just boarded a plane in Newark that was bound for Chicago O'Hare Airport. I have a meeting at the Chicago Board of Trade on Wednesday, December 8, 1996 at 9:30 Central time. I remember giving my ticket to the flight attendant outside the ramp to the plane, when the following happen to me.

It was July 1963. My brother Richie and I are sitting in the kitchen with our mother Grayce. Our mom was talking about her plans to go shopping in New York City for the day. My mom was on the phone with her sister Josephine, trying to see if Aunt Josephine could watch Richie and me for a few hours while she went shopping. Aunt Jo was my mom's younger sister. She was still single, but was engaged to be married soon. She was a carefree, fun person; we always loved being around her. Once, when she was watching me, I threw a soda bottle in the back yard and forgot all about it. Eventually, as the day went by, I was running around barefoot and stepped on the broken bottle and cut the bottom of my foot wide open. The cut required twenty-five stitches and almost made my aunt and mom pass out. Unfortunately, Aunt Josephine was working today at the bowling alley and could not watch us. Aunt Jo felt terrible; she loved to watch us and always had fun playing games or just walking to the park. My mom called her mother, our grandmother Filomena, to see if she could watch us. My grandmother couldn't watch us either; she had plans to play bingo with her friends. Grandma didn't get out much. She had a bad back and was considered a cripple. She never made plans for the day, except for this day. Before I was born, she had a major operation on her spine; the doctor from the Brooklyn Dodgers performed the experimental operation. My mom let Grandma off the hook, because Grandma would've cancelled if my mother pushed her a bit. My mom didn't know what to do; she was planning this day in New York City for a couple of weeks. Klein's on 14th Street was having a big one-day sale and she didn't want to miss it.

I remember this day very clearly. My mom thought about taking my brother and me, but she didn't want to drag us in and out of the department stores all day. We never liked shopping, watching a bunch of ladies running around the store grabbing as much clothing as they could to take into the dressing room to try on; that would be boring. Watching someone diving into the pile of bargain dresses was entertaining though. My mom decided to take a chance and bring Richie and me along with her with the hope she could find her dad, our grandfather (Papa Jim). Papa Jim just happens to drive a New York City bus. His route went cross town west to east on 14th Street.

We all headed down to the F train on McDonald Avenue in Brooklyn. This was called the independent line. The train line ran on the el, (short for elevated train). Forty-five minutes later, the F train pulled into 14th Street Union Square Station. The subway platform was jammed with people standing, waiting to board and people walking in different directions, going about their own business. This was the first time I had taken the train into Manhattan that I could remember. The doors of the train opened up and people started charging out just as soon as people started rushing into the train. Our mom held onto our arms so tightly that it seemed we were being lifted off our feet and pulled through the crowd. I actually enjoyed the journey through the crowd, dodging in and out of groups of gathering commuters, shoppers, and tourists.

Up the subway stairs and onto the streets of New York City, 14th Street was so busy, people and cars filled the sidewalks and streets. Our mom told us to keep our eyes open for New York buses coming from either direction. So my brother and I were staring west and east on 14th Street, looking for a bus to appear. We saw a bus a few avenues away; it seemed like it was standing still. Finally, the bus approached the bus stop. Richie and I on cue started waving frantically. The nice, polite bus driver pulled up opened the door and waved back to us a wink and drove off. The bus driver must've felt terrible when our response was not one of joy but great disappointment. He was not actually what we were expecting.

The next bus that came along had a familiar-looking white-haired man driving. We started waving to the driver. The bus pulled over to the curb immediately and opened the front doors. My brother Richie and I looked up and were shocked to see Papa Jim with his usual big smile on his face. Our mom didn't have to say a word. Our grandfather knew exactly what she needed him to do for her. "Dad, I'll see you in a couple of hours on this corner, and thank you," my mother said.

Richie and I are on the bus, sitting right behind Grandfather. We have these great big smiles on our faces and are very excited to be riding the bus with our grandfather.

The bus travels up and down 14th Street for an hour or so, when in a manner completely typical of our grandfather, he ventures to say, "I'm hungry. What about you boys?" As we get closer to the West Side, the bus makes a sharp right-hand turn and heads uptown a couple of blocks. The bus pulls up in front of a diner.

Grandpa Jim, Richie, and I walk off the bus and into the diner. Tessy the waitress looks up at our grandfather and says, "Half a day today, James?"

"No, just taking a detour to get something to eat. My boys came into New York today just to be with their grandfather. What do you think of that, Tessy?" My brother and I look at each other, shrug our shoulders and smile.

Grandpa orders the usual, two hamburgers, two chocolate shakes for us, and of course, the same for him. We are hungry and we eat everything on our plates.

My grandfather looks at his watch and jumps up. His smile and relaxed demeanor has turned to panic, and his mouth now wide open, he shouts, "We have to go! We have to go!" as he jumps from the counter. "Tessy, I'll pay you later in the week, I got to go."

We rush onto the bus. Grandpa starts the bus and off we go. The bus makes a wild U-turn on the West Side Highway. People in their cars are beeping their horns and yelling at my grandfather from out of their car windows. Richie and I are in shock and we have this look of horror on our faces while our grandfather is laughing out loud. Back on 14th Street, the bus pulls up to the bus stop. There seems to be a longer line at the bus stop than usual. As the people start to board the bus, our grandfather is introducing everyone to us. Not everyone is so pleased to meet us, especially since they have been waiting for a bus for over thirty minutes.

A couple of trips across 14th Street and everything seems to be back to normal. My grandfather tells my brother Richie to jump up on his lap and help him drive the bus. Richie jumps up on his lap without the slightest hesitation. I look up at my grandfather with a slight frown on my face. My grandfather hands me the change maker that usually hangs on his belt. He tells me "I need you to give change to the passengers for me."

My frown instantly turns into a great big smile. "Really, Grandpa; I can give change to everyone?"

At that point, my grandfather asked me, "Oh by the way, can you count?"

"Yes, to 100, I think."

"Great, you're hired," declares my grandfather.

Hours later, my mother showed up on the corner of 14th Street and Union Square with her arms full of shopping bags. "That looks like Mom," declares my brother Richie.

"How can you tell?" I asked.

"I can see her dark black hair and hat she was wearing." Grandpa Jim pulls the bus over to the curb. At that point, we jump off the bus and run to help our mom with her bags. Richie and I turn around to say good-bye to Grandpa Jim, and just like when he pulled up to the curb in the morning, with a great big smile on his face, he waves good-bye, drives off, and shouts, "See you at home later!"

My brother and I had the most memorable day two boys could ever have had with a grandfather and Mother. This is the third time in my life that I have relived this event. I jumped back to December 8, 1996, my seat and name is being announced on the overhead speakers to report to Gate 26 immediately.

The year is 1963 in New York and 1996 in Newark Airport.

*Grandma Filomena
and Grandpa Jim*

74

Chapter 14

Kokomo Clowns

The day was December 22, 2001. It was an extremely cold winter day for December. I heard on the radio there was chance of snow. I was driving to see my daughter Monique; things weren't great between us. I was going through a divorce, in fact a very nasty divorce. I was feeling a lot of pressure from lawyers, ex-wife, and work. I was working for Con Edison, and was not very satisfied with what I was doing. I just accepted a severance package from Global Crossing/IXNet. I loved my job at IXNet; I enjoyed traveling, I enjoyed the people I worked with, a lot of them I considered my friends, and some of them like Michelangelo and Chris, I considered my family. I missed the corporate environment, business class, boring boardroom meetings, and Europe. I loved traveling to Europe; I spent a few months a year in London and some time in Germany, and if I traveled with Michelangelo, Sicily was on our destination. Michelangelo and I would always find time to sneak out of London and catch a flight to Rome, and then shuttle down to Cimmina, Sicily, his home town, which is about twenty minutes from Cefalu, which is where my Grandma Prestipino was from. These were great times, visiting Michelangelo's sister Josephine and husband Mimo in Sicily. Meeting Michelangelo's Italian friends and family was like traveling back in time, a wonderful time and era. I guess I have been thinking about that a lot. I also have my daughter Monique on my mind. Monique and I have had a great relationship. We were so close since the day she was born and spent so much time together. She was a perfect child; she did everything I enjoyed. I took her to baseball games, tailgate parties for the Giants, the racetrack. She played every sport I played growing up, except for equestrian, which I have to say I enjoyed watching the most. I know I have to talk to her and without saying too much let her understand why things are the way they are right now. I stayed in the marriage longer than I should have, mainly because of Monique. This was hard for her to understand. I believe she thought I abandoned her. I guess in a way I did; there was no easy way to leave. I lost a few million dollars of company stock that there was no chance of ever recovering. So I was feeling stressed and a little depressed over my career and personal life. My relationship with Janet was getting stronger; I had strong feelings for her and she for me. But Janet thought I should take things slower and get my life in order. So add all this up and I'm a very confused person. I haven't time traveled in a while. Usually when I'm worried or stressed, I jump, or time travel, whatever way you want to reference it. I'm still not sure what to consider it.

So here I am driving along the parkway, and before you know it, I'm standing in a baseball uniform on a baseball field. The weather is hot and the sun is directly overhead, shining down strong. I look around and I can see the stadium is full to capacity; people are sitting and standing everywhere. There must be at least 10,000 people in this small ballpark.

"Hey you, hey kid, get over here. We need you to run the bases and slide into second when we tell you to."

I looked over at the voice and in a whisper I replied, "Who, me? You want me?"

"Yes," the coach yelled back, "yes you."

I throw my glove to the side and trot over to first base. As I'm trotting over to the base, I notice the players in the field are dressed in uniforms but resemble clowns. Their cap has a big clown face on the front and the uniform has Kokomo Clowns written across it. I can't believe my eyes. I'm somewhere in New Hampshire; the year is probably 1940-something, I'm not sure. Immediately I started to look for my dad. He's got to be here, why else am I here? There's a couple of guys tossing the ball around, playing a fancy game of pepper, throwing the ball over their heads, around their bodies, doing acrobatics. Over comes this coach in a regular uniform and asks me, "Do you know what to do?" I begin to say no and he replies, "Ok, when I tell you to take off, you run as hard as you can toward second base."

"What do I do when I get to second base?"

"Don't worry, you'll be fine!" he shouts back to me.

All of a sudden, as clear as day, like a fantasy come true, my eyes can't believe it, my mouth opens wide. I see him, there he is, young, strong, handsome, tall, lean, muscular. How else can I explain him? My dad running out onto the field to take his position. I can't take my eyes off of him. My dad would tell me stories of his years on the road with Kokomo Clowns, playing baseball against semi-pro and minor league teams in the

New England states . He would tell me about the crowds and how it was so exciting to put on a performance for the crowd and then play a baseball game afterwards.

"Go! GO! I said GO!!!" The coach was yelling for me to go, "Run, take off," he screamed. I looked back at him and immediately started running. I was about three-quarters of the way to second. I wasn't slowing up, I didn't know if I should run right through the base, slide, barrel over my dad, who I can see a lot clearer now straddling second base, looking like he was waiting for the ball to arrive. I see him so clearly, that smile, that smile he always had; he seemed amused, couldn't understand why. All of a sudden, as I am picking up speed, my uniform pants flew off, as if there was a string attached to them. I stumbled, tripped, and tumbled the rest of the way towards second base. When I finally came to a stop and the cloud of dust settled, I was a good six feet in front of second base. I stood up and immediately looked around. All 10,000-plus people in the stadium were laughing and applauding uncontrollably. My pants were below my ankles. I was standing in boxer underbriefs that were five sizes too big and seemed to have cushion stuffed inside. I froze; I must've had a look of horror on my face. I take my attention from the sellout crowd for a second and look back towards second base. There is my dad, standing on the base with a devilish smile on his face. His legs kind of crossed as he has one foot flat and his other crossed with his toe on the bag. He's flipping the ball in the air a foot or so, taunting me that he is waiting for me. I panic again. I turn around to run back to first; he takes off towards me. I fall, of course, because my pants are around my ankles. I jump to my feet once again, and sure enough, there is another player standing in front of me. He has that same devilish smile on his face, doing the same thing as my dad was, flipping the ball, taunting me to run again. Finally, finally I get it; I know what is happening. This is not a bad dream or a nightmare, I am part of the show, I may be the star of the show, for all I know. Now would be a good time to wake up, jump, or time travel, whatever it is I'm doing. As luck has it, I'm not going anywhere, I'm stuck in a pickle; specifically, I am in a baseball pickle with a bunch of baseball players dressed as clowns running me back and forth, my pants around my ankles, and 10,000 people laughing hysterically. My dad shouts to me, "You're doing great, kid. I love the look on your face. Keep it going, and run towards me."

I take his cue and begin to run. This time, I grab my pants from below my ankles and lift them up in my hands and hold them near my chest and take off towards second base again. This time I have my sights on second base and I intend on sliding into the bag safe. I happen to be an excellent slider; of course I am, and I think I know why; my father taught me how to slide. As I reach the base, I throw my legs up and become airborne toward second base. I slide into second base with a cloud of dust and dirt. As the dust settles, I can still hear the crowd roaring with laughter, even more than earlier. I should've known they weren't going to let me slide into second base safe. I just had that feeling that I was not going to like what the final result was. As I jumped to my feet, I look around and down to the ground. To my surprise, or should I say, not to my surprise, second base is still about ten feet away from where I slid so skillfully. Of course, why not? It makes perfect sense, a trick second base, one that moves. My dad and his teammates at this point are bent over and laughing so loud. All I can hear is "great slide, kid, you're doing great, kid. Who is this kid?" Then my dad came over and asked me "Where you learn how to slide like that, kid?"

I couldn't help myself. I started laughing along with everyone on the field. I picked up my pants and trotted off the field with the Kokomo Clowns, to the sound of a standing ovation from the visiting teams' fans.

Back in the dugout all the guys came over and started patting me on the head and back, congratulating me on my surreal performance.

My dad looked at me as he always does during these time travels; "have we met before," or "you look very familiar." Sometimes I would get the feeling that he knew who I was, but he wasn't going to be the one to say it.

Hi dad, hey dad, it's me. As I look to the right, there is Monique, standing on the passenger side of my car, which is parked in the driveway of my house. "Aren't you going to let me in?"

"Of course I am. Get in, sweetheart."

Monique got in the car. "Dad, you ok? You look a bit flustered, you sure you're feeling all right?"

"I'm doing excellent, my dear. I couldn't feel better, really; thanks for asking, though."

Kokomo clowns 1940-something, what a game, my moment of fame, so to speak.

Chapter 15

Capri

Italy is the most beautiful country in the world, as far as I'm concerned. The country landscape, history, the strong customs, and the people are magnificent. Italians have a way of making American Italians feel so at home. When you visit friends or family in Italy, they really do treat you great. Not like in the States, where our first reaction is to say we're too busy to spend quality time with our guest from Italy. It's a big inconvenience, we have to cook for them or drive them into New York City, park the car, and walk around looking at the same skyscrapers we work in every day. They all want to visit Ellis Island, which for Italians should be a sacred place, due to all the Italian immigrants who travel through the island. When Americans go over to Italy, the Italians make themselves available; they sincerely welcome you. They make time to drive you everywhere, and if you forget to visit a relative or friend, they get highly insulted. I've always considered myself Italian, until the very first time I visited Sicily. My first visit to Italy was with my good friend Michelangelo. Michelangelo's family lives in Sicily. His parents spend part of the year in Sicily and the other half of the year in Rockland County. In fact, Michelangelo's sister Josephine lives in Sicily. Josephine and Michelangelo were born and raised in Rockland County, but spend many summers vacationing in their families' villas in Sicily. Their grandparents still live in the small town of Cimmina. Cimmina is a small village about twenty minutes outside of Palermo and half of the people in the town are related to the Graziano family. Michelangelo's family name is Graziano. His family is the warmest, nicest group of people you can ever meet. I have a great connection with the Graziano family. Josephine met her husband Mimo during one of her summer trips to Sicily and has lived in Cimmina since she was married over twenty years ago. Josephine and Mimo have a few homes in Cimmina.

They have a traditional village home located in the middle of the town, a beautiful villa on the outskirts of the town, this house they live in year-round, and they have an absolutely breathtaking 200-year-old country home overlooking the olive fields and mountain views of Sicily.

Michelangelo and I were in London on a business trip, we were meeting with a company named Credit Swiss First Boston, and they were headquarters in London. We arrived in London on Monday morning, and had scheduled some business meeting with a few brokerage firms in London.

We had a dinner planned with a few people from Credit Swiss First Boston to discuss what we were going to present on Tuesday morning.

That night, we went out to dinner at a restaurant called Chaz Niko, supposedly the restaurant was own by a famous chef in London, Chaz Niko. Chaz Niko was a very chichi place, and we had to generously tip the hotel concierge for this reservation. One of the funniest moments in a restaurant was with Michelangelo. We were anxiously awaiting appetizers and entrees. Our English friends were raving about this restaurant all evening. The waiter brought out a bowl of soup to Michelangelo. Michelangelo looked at the bowl of soup in front of him, from there on the scene was hilarious; the bowl of soup was no bigger than an espresso cup. The look on Michelangelo's face was priceless; he picked up his spoon, which was obviously not the correct spoon for this cup of soup, and attempted to put the spoon into the cup of soup. The spoon was too big for the cup and didn't fit. Watching him look around the table with a bewildered expression on his face was great. I was trying not to laugh, but when he looked at me, he instantly snapped at me, "Don't say a word; I don't want to hear your opinion, shut up, right now, not one word."

I couldn't help myself, I just burst into laugher. "Hey Michael, how's your soup? Looks great, maybe you can save me some."

"Very funny, you're a comedian." He explains to our guest, "Yeah, my buddy Gary is a very funny person. You know what?" Michelangelo said, "Why don't you have my soup, I'm not that hungry at the moment."

"Are you sure Michael?"

"Yeah, I'm very sure. Here, go ahead, enjoy. Maybe you can save me some," he laughed sarcastically.

He passed the soup over to me; I picked up the small espresso-size cup of soup and downed it in one gulp. The entire table laughed except for Michelangelo. The evening was evolving into one laugh after another. The lamb chops came out, or should I say lamb chop, as in the singular. If you thought the soup was small, the lamb chop was literally two inches long. The table roared when the waiter put the single lamb chop down in front of Michelangelo. At this point, Michael was also playing it up good for our business guest. Michelangelo and I have this way of playing off each other; our clients always seem to enjoy it. We were once out to dinner with three beautiful French ladies who worked at the French Embassy. When Michelangelo stepped away from the table, I explained to our three dinner companions that Michelangelo was a very popular American actor, but that he was very shy about his fame. When Michelangelo returned to the table, the three girls couldn't stop staring at him. "Ok, ok what did he say? What did he say about me?" The girls started giggling and one of them politely asked him to sign her menu. Michelangelo looks over to me. "Ok who am I now?"

I replied, "No one, just Michelangelo Graziano, very successful telecommunication sales executive, nice guy," and in a much lower mumbled voice I whispered: "famous Hollywood actor."

"I told you not to tell anyone about me. Young ladies, I apologize for my friend, he speaks too much when he should be minding his own business. I prefer to keep my status unknown, I will sign your menus, but please treat me as a normal person." Michelangelo could play it up real good. And one last thing he says, "You, Gary my dear friend, in the future, please keep your comments and childish behavior to yourself."

Back at Chaz Niko, the tab for our dinner came, and the bill was over 1,500 US dollars. Michelangelo was picking up the tab; he couldn't believe his eyes. He couldn't believe the final bill was so high. He couldn't resist the temptation of making a comment to the waiter, an already uptight English waiter. He wanted to see him squirm a bit. "So, where can I find a pizza parlor close by?"

"Excuse me, sir?"

"A pizza parlor, you know, pizza, real food. I'm so freaking hungry, I have to eat something."

Michelangelo paid the tab and very generously tipped the wait staff. This was classic Michelangelo. After the dinner and a long night of drinking, Michelangelo and I went back to the hotel. We ordered grilled cheese sandwiches from the lobby dining room.

After we presented to our prospect and spent another night on the town entertaining the Englishmen, we drank beer, more beer, and then we had some more beer. In the taxi ride back to the hotel, Michelangelo announces to me, "Let's go to Italy."

The next day, we were on a first-class flight to Rome, Italy. We had dinner on the flight to Rome; Michelangelo swears it was the best meal he had all week, and he was probably right. From Rome, we transferred to a shuttle flight to Palermo, Sicily. Josephine picked us up at the Palermo airport and drove us to her villa in Cimmina. We spent five wonderful days in Sicily, driving along the countryside. Mimo drove us to my Grandma Mary's home town of Cefalu. Cefalu was a beautiful fishing village which has an icon of a church on the map of Sicily. The town is famous for their church, which has two huge light towers facing the ocean. Once in Cefalu, we looked up the address of a distant relative of my grandmother Mary, Cousin Anna was the niece of my grandmother's sister, I knocked on the door of the slightly run-down apartment villa. Anna's son opened the door, standing in front of us in his boxer shorts, tank top shirt, three-day beard, and looking very hung over from the night before. Michelangelo looked over at me and I gave him back the nod he was looking for. In Italian, Michelangelo excused himself that he was looking for a relative of the Marino family. Of course, the man at the door said he had no relatives named Marino. Michelangelo apologized and we left. We decided to look for a place to get some lunch. We found a charming little restaurant on the water. We walked into the restaurant; there was no one eating lunch at this time, so we sat down at table overlooking the ocean and ordered linguine with black sauce. It was one of the best seafood meals I ever had. We spent most the day laughing at the sight of my distant cousin standing in the hall half-naked.

"Wait till we get back to the States and I tell everyone about your cousin," Michelangelo went on and on. Josephine and Mimo treated us so well; we met every relative and friend in town. At one point, Michelangelo and I walked in a procession for Saint Joseph Day through the heart of town. It was the week before Easter Sunday and the town was celebrating Saint Joseph Day in typical Italian style .Cimmina introduce me to the real Italy and a better understanding of what Italian people are really like in their homeland. We're used to the Italian Americans in Brooklyn; I don't consider myself Italian-American anymore. I am American from Italian descent and feel a deep connection to the country.

I visited Italy on a second occasion with my daughter Monique, niece Kristina, and my ex-wife. Again we traveled through Sicily, with stops in Cimmina, Cefalu, Frank Villa, Taroimia, and Capri. Monique and Kristina wanted to see the house their great-grandma Prestipino was born in. So we walked all around the town till I came upon this beautiful villa near the sea. The door and windows were painted with beautiful greens, reds, and yellows, flowers adorned the windowsills, potted plants were placed all around the courtyard. It was beautiful. "This is it," I announced, "this is Great-grandma Prestipino's house where she was born."

The girls were mesmerized by the sight. "Wow, this is beautiful, Uncle Gary."

"Dad, I just love it here," said Monique. I took a few pictures of the house, broke off a few flowers, and off we went. The girls just loved it, the sights, our heritage, the food; it was truly a wonderful trip. It was very rewarding to see how the girls took in all the sights and traditions; they were enjoying the country and learning about their Italian heritage. The girls were able to venture out on their own in Capri; it was very safe and their was no way off the island but the ferry .

My latest trip to Italy came in 2003; Monique just started her freshman year at Fordham University. I helped Monique get settled into her dorm and to begin a new phase in her life, college. I knew she would do great; she was a straight-A student four years straight at Red Bank Catholic and she was just beginning to recognize her talents and was ready to peak.

Janet and I are going to Italy; we have been planning this for two months now. We waited till September, to get Monique settled into college and then we were going to Italy to get married.

It felt so right; Janet is from Italian descent as well as I, and Janet also traveled to Italy on a few occasions. Janet was in the travel business for over twenty years and she has been all over the world.

We have been planning a civil ceremony to take place in Capri. We hired a wedding planner to help assist us with the paperwork and to stand up for us. I was very fortunate that Janet is a lot like me; she was not looking for the traditional wedding and reception. So one day, while we were talking about Italy and what a beautiful place Capri is, we decided to get married in Capri. WOW, how were we going to pull this off? Janet just loved the idea of doing something different and was very excited about marrying me in Italy. I too was very excited; I could barely wait to get to Italy. I knew this was so right, that we were meant to be together, and that Janet was to be my wife. The best was to come. We landed in Naples and immediately went to the American Consulate to get our marriage certificate. Piera our wedding planner picked us up at the airport and chauffeured us around. We were unable to get all the paperwork completed that day, but Piera was able to go back to Naples and take care of it all for us, without us being there. Janet and I spent the first day in Capri relaxing at the beach. It was September and the weather was gorgeous. This summer was so brutally hot in Italy, the temperatures were well into the 100s for most of July and August. In fact, Janet lost two aunts to the heat that summer. Her aunts lived in a neighboring island called Isca and had passed away from heatstroke.

Our fifteen minutes of fame began about 4:30 PM on September 5th. I met Janet at the hotel; she came walking down the stairs in a beautiful white dress. She looked like a Hollywood movie star right out of a romance novel. I stopped and stared at her; she looked nervous. I walked up to her, kissed her gently, and said, "I love you very much. You have nothing to be nervous about. I will take care of you forever. I want you to be my wife and life partner. Now let's go get married."

I hired a photographer to take pictures of the wedding, before and after. If you've ever been to Capri, you'll know there are no cars allowed at the top of Capri Island. Our hotel was at the point of the island, so that meant we had to walk from the hotel to the mayor's office in the main square plaza. We began our long walk through the narrow streets of Capri. As we passed outdoor cafes, clothing stores, tourists, and townspeople, everyone was telling us in Italian: "AGOODA, AGOODA" which in English means BEST WISHES. We walked through crowds of people while the two photographers snapped photos of us. It was the greatest feeling in the world; I have never been the center attention for anything in my life. Now today I was walking through the streets of Capri with the most beautiful woman by my side, the woman I love, and want to marry. I was happy, and I knew Janet, who is also a very private person, was enjoying this sudden fame and celebrity. We arrived at the mayor's office and walked up the stairs to his office. The mayor was waiting for us; he was dressed in a grey suit and was wearing a huge, colorful band across his chest. The ceremony was spoken in Italian and translated to Janet and me in English. It was a beautiful ceremony. The mayor, I believe, had a connection with Janet and me. I think he liked that we were both of Italian descent. Janet's last name was Signoretto and mine is Prestipino. Mayor Frederic went on and on about how happy he was for us and what a wonderful couple we were, and how he wished us much happiness, health, and love forever.

After the ceremony, we walked back out into the square, where a crowd had gathered to throw rice on us and again wished us best wishes (Agooda).

Janet and I spent the next five beautiful days enjoying the Capri sun, lounging on the beach, swimming in the ocean, watching and enjoying the people of Capri, eating in the restaurants in town and in the mountains of Anna Capri. Capri is situated on the top of the mountain on this little island. The views from the top of Capri are just breathtaking; it is one of the great wonders of the world. We loved Capri, but we were ready to leave, to take the ferry back to the mainland and spend some time in another romantic spot called Positano, Amalfi Coast. The hotel in Positano was magnificent; we had a suite with a twenty-by-twenty balcony overlooking the ocean. At night, the ocean would blow a cool breeze through our curtains and into our room. In the morning, if I awoke early, I would watch the fishermen from my balcony preparing and untangling their fishing nets for the day, to throw into the ocean. Janet and I hired a driver and toured the Amalfi Coast. We relaxed, walked the streets of this quaint seaside town, shopped, and enjoyed our first days as husband and wife.

Sometimes when my life is filled with complications and the stress of running a company, being a father, a son, and husband, and I feel like I can't go on, I just close my eyes and picture Positano, Capri, Janet and me, and I'm right back there, reliving my dream. In my life, there have been two wonderful events that will forever be in my heart: the birth of my daughter Monique and the day I married my wife Janet.

Janet and I getting married in Capri

Michelangelo and me in Sicily

Janet and I in Positano

Chapter 16

Milk trucks do tip

The year is 1985. It's September 15, almost a year after my daughter Monique was born. Things are going well for me. I'm starting a new job at a company named TRT, which stood for Tropical Radio and Telegraph. An engineer I work with at Sprint introduced me to a VP of strategic planning at TRT. It was a whole new world for me. I've been a technician for almost ten years and now I was moving into a product development/sales role. Heck, I didn't own a suit or an overcoat. In fact, the first year, I wore just a suit jacket all winter. I froze. I used to run from the office to the subway and to the bus that would take me home. It also was the first time I was introduced to traveling to work in a city other than New York. Twice a week, I caught the Big Apple Airline shuttle from Newark to Washington DC.

I haven't jumped in quite a while. I guess I've been too busy and my mind is cluttered with new and challenging responsibilities. A daughter who just makes me melt every time I see her, my mind is full of her voice, image, and smile. I love being a father; it's the most satisfying experience ever. My daughter Monique has been so wonderful; she has changed my life and made me look at things differently. I've become a better person and respect life and people more now, maybe because I'm so grateful for having her in my life. Well, back to my story. It was September 15, 1985. I was in a boardroom with a bunch of executives at 1331 Pennsylvania Avenue Washington, DC. My boss is talking about a new product we're rolling out and all of a sudden, I'm sitting on a horse-drawn wagon. It's dark, cold, actually very cold, and the wagon is moving very fast through some cobblestone street. I start to look around to see if I recognize where I am. I know I'm not in Washington DC anymore. I hope they don't miss me too much in my board meeting. It looks like I'm in downtown Brooklyn.

The reason I know it's downtown Brooklyn is because Brooklyn Heights hasn't changed much since the 1920s or so. The streets are cobblestone, the factories are very old, and the renovations have kept up with the look of that era. There is a young man sitting next to me on the wagon. He is, of course, driving the wagon and controlling the reins. Wow, its cold. I am literally shaking with chill from head to toe. The young man next to me looks very familiar. He is slightly tall for this era, with a slim build, he has thick, jet-black hair so long that it falls in front of his eyes. He looks over at me and smiles. At that very moment, I know who he is. I can't believe it, that same smile, those dark eyes, that carefree, easygoing demeanor . I instantly know where I am, I've heard this story many times before. Here I am somewhere in the 1920s, sitting on a horse-drawn wagon with a few hundred gallons of fresh milk behind me. Not that I can see the milk, but I know it's there. "Boy is it cold," I said to the young man next to me. Again he just looks over and smiles.

"Hold on," he says, "we're going over the Brooklyn Bridge to Manhattan." I knew he was going to say that; I've heard this story before. The young man next to me is my grandfather, Vincent Palame, nicknamed Jim for some reason. I can't believe it, my grandfather Jim is sitting right next to me, driving the horse-drawn milk truck wagon. My grandfather turned to me and asked me, "How do you like your new job, is it what you expected?"

I had to think for a minute, I know he's not talking about my job in DC. Or maybe he is. Of course not, he doesn't know me from a hole in the wall. "I'd like it a lot better if it wasn't so cold," I replied.

My grandfather started laughing; figures, just like he is now as an older person, oblivious to the cold and circumstances. I just spoke to him today, or should I say sixty years later, during my break from our meeting. Same laugh, same easygoing ways. "Don't worry, you'll get used to it. The cold is good for the milk. My name is James Palame. I didn't get your name earlier."

I looked at him and thought for a while. Oh well, does it matter, I said to myself. "Gary Prestipino, Gary Prestipino," I said twice.

"Nice to meet you, Mr. Gary Prestipino. Interesting name there you have, my new friend; we're going to get to know each other real well." I started to laugh; all of a sudden, I didn't feel that cold anymore, and I was actually starting to relax.

I replied to Jim, "Yes, we're going to know each other real well, I'm sure of it." As we began to make our approach toward the Brooklyn Bridge, my relaxed mood quickly turned to fear. I remember this story, my grandfather has told me this story a dozen times, a cold winter night, milk truck wagon, pulled by two horses.

I have to do something; this is not good, I know what happens next. "Grandpa, be careful, are these horses going too fast?"

"What did you say? Grandpa? I'm about the same age as you are, my friend." He laughed as he always does. "Don't worry, we need to get these ponies moving to make it over the bridge." All of a sudden it seemed like the horses were in a race with each other as they began to make the climb up the bridge grade to get over the ice cold bridge. As the horses raced toward the top of the bridge, I could see that they were bumping against each other. I learned from my daughter Monique that horses love the cold and they usually get a little jumpy, love to cantor and run in the cold weather.

The wagon began shaking from side to side, and I found myself holding on for my life. I glanced over at my young grandfather and could see for the first time that he no longer had that trademark smile of my grandpa Jim anymore. He was fighting hard to control the horses, but they were not responding to him. No sooner had he yelled to me to hold on, than the wagon behind us rocked so much from side to side that it actually turned sideways and was sliding forward on the ice. At this point, the horses were not running anymore, but sidling almost like in an animated cartoon way, feet down, stiff, like stepping on a break. And then it happened; the milk truck tipped over, my grandfather and I went flying, the horses disconnected from the wagon and continued over the bridge to the Manhattan side. Grandpa and I were lying under the upside-down milk truck.

Grandpa yelled over to me, "You ok, Gary, you, are you OK!"

I was on the Brooklyn Bridge, right in the middle of one of my grandfather's stories. All of a sudden, I started laughing. "Yes, I'm ok, how about you?" There was milk everywhere, hundreds of broken bottles of milk. My grandfather looked over at me and he too started laughing uncontrollably.

"I guess I'll have to look for a new job. Maybe the transportation business is not for me."

I looked over at him and said, "Maybe the milk delivery business is over for you, but not transportation." He just smiled and laughed some more.

"Gary, so what do you think? Should we go with London to New York service and what should we name it?" I was back. I'm not sure how long I was gone and how much I missed, but I was back. My boss was talking as he usually was, and was looking for approval.

I stuttered slightly, and said "City Direct, YES, let's call it City Direct. Let's show a photo of the Brooklyn Bridge and London Bridge and market it as bridging the two countries together. What better bridges than the Brooklyn Bridge in New York and the London Bridge in London?" Everyone at the table went quiet for a moment.

"Great idea, great idea!" shouted my boss Rich. "City Direct is our new product name."

My grandfather told me this story of him and a brand new apprentice driver in route to deliver milk to New York's Wall Street one winter night, and how he flipped the milk truck over on the Brooklyn Bridge. I always believed the story because it was typical of my grandfather to be in the middle of a stressful position, and the fact he could actually laugh about was definitely his style.

What a night, milk and memories everywhere!

Brooklyn Bridge, New York

Chapter 17

Teenage in Brooklyn

Being a teenager in Brooklyn was a great experience for me; I learned so much about life, good and bad, from the streets of the City. Every neighborhood in Brooklyn had its own group of interesting people. I knew my share and quite a few from the other neighborhoods as well. When you're a teenager living in Brooklyn, you hang around the school yard or a typical city concrete park. I remember playing in one of those concrete parks (today they have rubber mats around all the swings and slides), when I was about seven years old. I was climbing up the slide the wrong way, when I was startled by my dad yelling to get down. I did immediately; I fell from the top and landed face-first on the concrete. My dad came running over to me and began yelling at me some more, "I told you not to climb up that slide, now see what happened!" All the way to the hospital he was telling me what I did. I knew what I did; I cut my chin wide open. The cut required twelve stitches. When I got home from the hospital, my grandmother and mom were waiting for me at the door. Of course, as soon as I walked in, I started crying, "He yelled and cursed at me, he yelled at me all the way to the hospital!" I cried out. My grandma, stunned, looked over at my mom and without hesitation, my mom said to my grandma, "I'll handle this, Mom." I know my mom gave my dad a earful that afternoon. I'm sure my dad did not get dinner that night. If you knew my dad, you would feel terrible for him. He was the kindest, gentlest father you would ever want to have. In all fairness to my dad, he probably panicked when he saw all that blood and didn't know what else to do, and it also happened on his watch.

My grandma never had to leave the house to go shopping. She had a person who came to the house to sell eggs and milk, a soda man, a fruit and vegetable man, a guy who sold house dresses, shoes, and jackets, and even the Good Humor man made sure he stopped and rang the bell before he passed our house. It was possible that one day you would walk out of your house and ten other kids on the block were wearing the same winter coat, compliments of some longshoreman who lived on our block and worked on the docks.

One day when I was about eleven years old, I decided to climb up onto PS 121's roof. The school was having brick work done to the chimney, which faced the inside of the school yard. The workers had built a scaffold all the way up the chimney to the roof of the school. So I began to climb the scaffold to the top. The older guys hanging out in the school yard were yelling up at me, "You're going to get in trouble, little Tito, you're not going to be able to get down once you get up there." I ignored them because I knew I would be able to get back down. I wasn't scared of heights, I've climbed the elevated train stations many times and they were a lot higher than the school. Up on the roof of the school, I could see the whole neighborhood; I walked over to the front of the school, where I could see my house clear as day. I could see my grandfather sitting on the stoop in front of our house. I saw my dad walking home from the train station; he was getting home from work. I knew any minute, my mom would be coming out on the stoop and yelling for my brother and me to come home to eat dinner. I waited on the roof to see my mom come out and call for me. I didn't hear her call Richie. I guess Richie was already home. As soon as I heard my mom call, I walked back to the school yard side of the building. I started to back myself off the roof and onto the scaffold to begin my climb back down. I took a few steps down, when all of a sudden, rocks were whizzing past my head. A couple rocks actually hit me in the leg and back. I held on real tight so as not to slip and fall four stories down. I hurried back up and onto the roof. I looked over the roof and yelled down, "What are you, crazy? You could've killed me." They were all laughing hysterically.

"I got to go home, my mom's calling me, let me down."

Joey Deleo, who was the toughest person in the neighborhood and who was good friends with my brother and family yelled back, "I told you you wouldn't be able to get back down." Brooklyn is where the cycle of life begins. The men pick on the big guys, the big guys pick on the older guys, and the older guys pick on me and my friends. Life's not always fair; eventually, it all evens out after you reach your twenties. The only thing that never evened out was Joey; you never went up against Joey, maybe out of respect. Who am I kidding, it was fear. Joey was always the man, just now we were friends and we could actually hang out together. I had many good times with Joey. He usually looked out for me. I'll tell you later on how he taught me a lesson about drinking.

Bobby Mugs, the Greek, and the priest were all down in the yard laughing up at me. Notice one thing: No one ever had a real name in the neighborhood. My street name was Gary the Ghost. When I was older, I had this way of avoiding trouble; when I saw trouble happening, I was gone. The next day, the guys would say, "What happened to you last night? So-and-so got arrested or someone got beaten up or worse, killed. This guy named Topper named me "the ghost," Topper was about forty-five years old and still hung out in the school yard. He never worked, he didn't have a car, he did nothing, just hung out every day.

I attempted to step back down off the roof when a new barrage of rocks was flying past my head once more. Back on the roof again, I'm begging the older guys to let me down. I was already at least forty-five minutes late for dinner. So I sat and waited, hoping they would go home and eat dinner with their own families or just get bored and leave. No such luck; they weren't going anywhere and either was I. Sure enough, to make matters worse, my dad walks into the school yard looking for me. I backed away from the ledge so my dad wouldn't see me. If he saw me on top of the roof, he would have killed me, and most likely every single older guy at the school yard. I know it was my chance to get down, but the consequences would be far worse than just getting home late. "Hey boys, you seen my son Gary?"

"Hey Mr. Prest, no, we haven't seen him all day."

"Well, if you do, please tell him to head home ASAP. He's late for dinner and his mom is worried about him."

"Ok, Mr. Prest, we'll be real sure to send him home if we see him."

"Good night, boys."

"Good night, Mr. Prest."

If this had happened today, my picture would already be on the 6 o'clock news. Another thing in Brooklyn, you never ran home and told your parents that one of the older guys roughed you up, took your money, or borrowed your bicycle for an undetermined time. It was rule and you followed it. I thought for sure they would let me down from the roof now that my father had just spoken to them. "Hey, Gary, you hear that? You got to go home, get down from there and get your ass home."

Thank God, I can finally get down from here and go home. As soon as I stepped on the scaffold, the rocks started hitting off the top of the building and falling down on me. Now I'm back on the roof and I'm crying. I won't let them know I'm crying, but I am. It was getting dark and I must have been on the roof for three hours now. Finally, my brother Richie walked into the school yard; he was sent out by my mom to find me. As soon as I saw him, I started screaming for him to help me.

"What the hell are you doing up there? Get the hell down here now, you moron."

"They won't let me come down. I've been trying for three hours and they keep throwing rocks at me."

Richie turned to the group of older guys, who were only about two or three years older than him, and he started yelling at them that they were effing idiots. "Get down here now!!" I backed off the roof and climbed my way back down the scaffold. I ran directly over to my brother to be consoled, and instead I got a smack on the head and boot in the ass. "Get home now and don't tell Mommy and Daddy you saw me. You better think of a good excuse by the time you get home."

As mad as Richie was with me, he would never sell me out to our parents. I saw worse things done to people who were getting a lesson taught to them — ears cut off, a baseball bat across the head. I saw these guys roll this kid who was wearing white overalls around freshly painted school doors. This kid had brown everywhere on his body.

I was walking home one afternoon from a friend's house and passing the bar on Avenue J and McDonald Avenue, when I heard Joey Deleo call my name from inside. "Gary, come in, I want to talk to you." I walked into the bar and Joey told me to sit up on the bar stool and hang out with him. Joey didn't like many of the young kids in the neighborhood much; he had no time for any of them. He liked me for some reason. It could've been because of my brother, or the fact I took everything he did to me without complaining. Once he had me drive him to another park about six blocks away on my bicycle. He got off my bike and actually said thank you. What was I thinking? I said "you're not welcome." I was hanging out with all my friends and he demanded I drive him, so I was a little pissed, to say the least. He kicked me right in the ass and then punched me twice in the head. I think that is when I started to learn how to survive. There's are a lot of dead tough guys from Brooklyn, but a real survivor knows when to walk away, when not to pick a fight, when to run, and never be a hero, unless it's for your family.

Joey ordered me a scotch. "Go ahead, down it quick." I did and it tasted terrible, like poison. Joey made me drink three more scotches, downing them all. He handed me a cigarette and I smoked my first cigarette. When I got off the bar stool, the room started to spin; I wasn't feeling very good. I was able to get home, but my mom took one look at me and said "You're drunk. What did you drink?" I interrupted her with my moaning that the room is spinning and I think I'm going to throw up. My mom was great. She knew I was sick and that yelling at me at this moment wasn't going to help the situation, so she just piled up a bunch of pillows and kept me sitting straight up.

A couple days later, Joey saw my mom and asked how I was feeling. My mom said "Better, why do you ask? Did you see him getting drunk?"

Joey said "Yes, I was teaching him a lesson on drinking."

"What lesson?" my mom asked.

"Drinking is bad for you."

My mom said "Why? Does Gary drink?"

Joey replied, "No, never, and he probably won't ever again." My mom was real mad at Joey and gave him a piece of her mind. She liked Joey and didn't hold a grudge against him, but did warn him about teaching me any more lessons.

I realized at an early age that drugs were bad for you, very bad, that is. I never took drugs; I just didn't see what the big thing was about them. Nodding out in front of your friends, not being alert, they weren't for me. Maybe the biggest reason for not taking drugs was because I was scared to; I didn't want to disappoint my parents. I'm not sure, maybe I'm not giving myself enough credit and I was a little smarter than I think I am. I knew a lot of people who took drugs, pills, smoked marijuana, and shot heroin. Eventually, later in life, I distanced myself from anyone doing drugs. I wrote them off my list of friends. I've had many friends and people I knew overdose from drugs. One night, this kid from my high school whose name was Billy was at the bowling alley and was drinking vodka from the bottle and taking secondalls, which were considered downers. I did what I always did and disappeared.

The next morning, I was at the roller hockey rink, putting on my equipment and skates with a bunch of my friends, getting ready to play roller hockey, when this kid, Louie, walks into the park and then into the roller rink to announce to all of us that his cousin Billy overdosed and died last night. We all were taken aback by this news. Billy was a nice kid; we were in a few classes together and I liked him. Until last night, I didn't know he was into drugs and drinking. I was little shocked because he was a weightlifter and I thought weightlifters were not drug users. After about ten minutes of all of us feeling bad and telling Louie to let us know when the wake was going to be held, we played hockey. We played hockey like nothing happened. For two hours we played hockey, roughed each other, got mad when the play didn't go our way. After the game, when I was changing into my clothes and sneakers, I couldn't help but think what a waste of a life Billy had. I'm sure his parents and family were going to feel terrible and miss him very much, but none of my friends, including me, really gave a damn about this kid overdosing on drugs and dying. I knew from that point on that I would always think of myself and family first. The neighborhood will always be there; no one really cares what happens to you besides your family and one or two close friends. That's why I never tried drugs, got involved in gang wars, or got a tattoo. Just about every one of my friends had a tattoo, which was good enough reason for me not to get one. When they had gang wars, the only person who ever got hurt was the innocent person, the person who didn't want to be involved, but couldn't say no. I never said no, I just walked away without being noticed. Hence, Gary the Ghost (survivor).

I can go on and on about Brooklyn stories. Maybe someday I'll put every Brooklyn story down in writing.

Being a teenager in Brooklyn taught me how to survive, not like you suspect, in the physical sense, but in the mind. Always think of the consequences, is anyone going to care if you were the hero of a stupid fight between two neighborhoods? If you're going to do something, then do it alone, not in front of everyone. Never let anyone know your scared of them, but do let them know you have fear, because fear creates action, and actions speak louder than words.

Final note from the author:

These are my stories, some of which are the stories of my life and my family history. I hope you enjoyed them as much as I did writing them in my journals. Like I've said many times before, I have been very lucky to be living this life, a life filled with many experiences. I've traveled throughout foreign countries, past and present, and for the most part, the ride has been great. I believe my life has been full and rewarding because of these experiences. Through these time travels, I have witnessed firsthand how my relatives' lives were before I was a thought in their minds. To see the beginning of a boy prematurely growing up, and the challenges of a brand new world, I'm able to appreciate my parents and grandparents more now. Not many people realize that their grandparents were once young, vibrant, and full of life and promise, and maybe they were just as irresponsible as you and I were, and didn't always do the proper things or act as you would expect them to. I have a great appreciation for history, and realize the foundation our ancestors built for the generations ahead. I can only hope the future generations are prepared for what lies ahead. I also know that no one is perfect; we all make mistakes, and we are entitled to change our minds. My views on life when I was younger are completely different than they are today. I have more respect for people than I did in the past. It doesn't hurt to treat someone equally and with dignity. Children are so important to the future, and if you can teach your kids one thing they can carry with them throughout their life, it should be to know your family, know how your great-grandparents lived their lives, where they emigrated from, what trade of work did they do, were they professional, or laborers, did they have an impact on the world, or did they just have a critical impact on you? Your family is part of history, and you should be proud to carry on your family name and to be a part of that family.

The End

Thanks to my family.

We will always remember you for eternity.

9 781425 915902